# REVOLUTION OR REFORM ?

Precedent Studies in Ethics
and Society.

Thomas E. Wren, *Editor of the series*

*Editor of this volume*
A. T. FERGUSON

*Translators*
MICHAEL AYLWARD
A.T. FERGUSON

*With an introductory essay by*
FREDERIC L. BENDER

# REVOLUTION OR REFORM?

## A Confrontation

HERBERT MARCUSE

and

KARL POPPER

*Editor of this volume*
A.T. FERGUSON

*Translators*
MICHAEL AYLWARD
A.T. FERGUSON

*With an introductory essay by*
FREDERIC L. BENDER

Precedent Publishing, Inc.
737 North Lasalle Street
Chicago, Illinois 60610
©1976 by New University Press
Second Printing 1985

Distributed by Transaction Books
New Brunswick (USA), Oxford (UK)

Text of the original German language edition, *Revolution oder Reform?* edited by Franz Stark 1972 by Kösel-Verlag, GmbH & Co., Munich. Published by permission.

Library of Congress Card Number: 75-12192
ISBN: 0-89044-020-4
Printed in the United States of America.

# CONTENTS

# NEW UNIVERSITY PRESS
# STUDIES IN ETHICS
# AND SOCIETY

## FOREWORD BY THE GENERAL EDITOR

This series provides a forum for the critical review of
enduring issues concerning ethics and society. This
approach can be either direct, as in the discussion
of skepticism in the present volume, or indirect, by
discussing the positions of classical philosophers on
these issues. In either case, however, the contributions
are selected and introduced by the editor in a way
most suitable for classroom use, either as a text-
book or a supplementary reading.

After a period of malaise within and beyond the
philosophical community, there is now fresh and
extensive interest in evaluating personal and institutional conduct. This series has been conceived in
response to this new interest, but its contents are not
to be regarded as if they had sprung fully formed
from the brow of Zeus. It intends to provide contri-
butors and readers alike with the opportunity for

fresh and innovative philosophical thinking, but at the same time it recognizes that we see farther when we stand "on the shoulders of giants"—in this case, those of the great ethical and social philosophers of this and earlier centuries. Hence each contribution in the series is both a review and a proposal. Students and other non-professional philosophers may be more interested in the review, whereas professional philosophers will probably be more interested in the proposal, but in each contribution proposal and review require each other in order to be fully understood.

THOMAS E. WREN

# MARXISM, LIBERALISM, AND THE FOUNDATIONS OF SCIENTIFIC METHOD

## Introductory Essay

*by*

## Frederic L. Bender

The text of the debate between Herbert Marcuse and Sir Karl Popper which follows in this volume raises many important issues. Although the informality of the original format gave neither thinker sufficient opportunity to present his position in its greatest strength and subtlety, the basic lines of Marcuse's neomarxian critical theory and Popper's naturalist liberalism are clearly outlined. The crucial issues between the two participants are (1) their anthropological-axiological positions with respect to the "nature" of man, society, and the practical functions of democracy as a mode of self-government; (2) the conceptions of science and of philosophy which lie behind each thinker's claims with respect to these; and (3) their respective conceptions of the means required and feasible for attaining their respective social goals. The remarks which follow will attempt to focus upon, and deal critically with, the problems implicit in these three areas.

It should be noted at the outset that the two frames of reference are mutually exclusive. Marcuse holds that late capitalist society, "the wealthiest and most technically advanced in history," both can and should offer "the greatest and most tangible opportunities for a peaceful and liberated human existence, but is instead a society that most efficiently represses these opportunities for peace and liberation."[1] Popper, on the other hand, sees all social orders of which we have any knowledge as containing "injustice and repression, poverty and destitution," but holds that in the contemporary western democracies these evils are combatted through representative democracy, the existence of certain political liberties, and the actions of the state itself. In Popper's opinion, these societies "are very imperfect and in need of reform, but they are the best ever." Marcuse contrasts late capitalist society with ideals of social existence and humanity which he believes can and should be achieved with the resources currently available. Popper, however, contrasts contemporary capitalist society with other contemporary societies and concludes in favor of the relative merits of the former. The argument which follows will demonstrate that the Marxian conception of social science regards the reduction of social phenomena to "facts" and "values" as a positivist abstraction having no legitimate place in social theory. It then follows that neither position represented in this "debate" is altogether satisfactory from a Marxist perspective— Popper's because of its ideological content, and Marcuse's because of the ideological form in which it is presented here.

## I. ANTHROPOLOGICAL-AXIOLOGICAL ASSUMPTIONS

### A. LIBERALISM

The first issue concerns Marcuse's and Popper's opposing conceptions of democracy, which in turn rest upon contrasting conceptions of man. Whereas the question of the nature and potential of man has been a leading theme of Marcuse's work, it has been generally lacking in Popper's. This is compensated by Popper's evident acceptance of the liberal assumptions about man, which have been enshrined in the ideology of the democracies which he is concerned to defend. The liberal conception of man, as found in such classical writers as John Locke, Adam Smith, Jeremy Bentham, John Stuart Mill and T.H. Green, rests upon the following assumptions:[2]

(1) Each individual is conceived as essentially separated from his fellows, related to them for common purposes only accidentally, temporarily, and for reasons of apparent utility to each individual. This is generally presented by liberal theorists as the claim that the only free social relations are contractual ones and that only a society based upon a contract by its members, or at least upon their tacit consent, can be a "just" society, that is, one in which men are "free" in the bourgeois sense.

(2) Each individual is seen as being essentially an egoist seeking to satisfy his needs and desires through acquiring utilities (use-values) as embodied in commodities. These needs and desires are themselves assumed to be infinite; that is, man is seen as a bundle of drives which lead him to consume utilities. Since these drives can never be satisfied but at most are only

temporarily satiated, and since the drives themselves may be multiplied without end, there is in principle no rational limit in this conception of human consumption. This irrationality, implying what was thought to be man's kinship to animals rather than to God, defined the novelty of the bourgeois ideology as contrasted with the late medieval world view. The market economy, or capitalism, even in its petty-commodity, pre-industrial form, which allows an individual who possesses commodities with exchange-value to choose his satisfactions from among all the use-values available, is held to be justified as (a) the economic basis of the "free" society; (b) providing incentive to maximize production for the sake of profit, which at least in principle is for the sake of consumption; and (c) allowing for the concentration of capital, which in turn fosters expanded production and increased profit.

(3)  Prior to the definitive triumph of the bourgeoisie over the feudal ruling classes, liberal theorists argued that the chief function of government was to apply force sufficient to coerce naturally rapacious egoists into desisting from mutual assault and plunder. This argument, implicit in Machiavelli and explicit in Hobbes, is still used by Popper, who remarks: "The state protects its citizens from brute force through legal and political institutions." Once bourgeois property and political relations were secured, liberal theorists, such as Locke, Thomas Jefferson and the framers of *The Rights of Man*, found it expedient to claim instead that the bourgeois rights of free disposal over one's own person, which is essentially the freedom to enter into contractual economic relations, and property, which was held to derive from one's person or from the labor which one "invests" in producing a commodity, are immutable and beyond legitimate infringement or usurpation by the state.

(4)   Insofar as it was generally assumed, at least from Adam Smith to the middle of the nineteenth century, that a market economy leads to the production of the maximum quantity of goods possible in any given set of circumstances, it was also held that a market economy is the most efficient (rational) economic system, as well as the most "just."

(5)   Finally, there is the further presupposition that if one has only one's labor-power to exchange for a wage, one cannot engage in remunerative work, no matter how socially necessary, unless one is allowed access to the means of production—that is, that one have a job. The distinction between socially necessary *work* and a *job* means that those who possess no commodities to exchange must enter into a labor contract with the owners of the means of production (the owners of capital) in order to receive the wage necessary to maintain their existence and that of their dependents. This implies that the owners of capital will exact a "price" from the laborer for allowing him to work, for they would have no motivation to make work available at the "risk" of their capital were it not to be profitable to them. This "price" exacted from the laborers is the extraction of surplus value, which is the defining characteristic of capitalist production.[3] The classical political economists' model of a society of petty commodity producers engaged in mutually beneficial exchange has never corresponded to the historical reality of capitalism, which has been based instead on the exploitation of wage labor, because there has never been a capitalist society in which all its members have had surplus commodities (other than labor-power) available for exchange. Furthermore, there must always exist in capitalism a class of persons who possess no exchangeable commodities except their labor-power, or

else there would be no wage labor and hence no industrial production. Now, the worker is "free" to work for this or that capitalist as he prefers, and he is even "free" to avoid work altogether. But insofar as this latter alternative usually leads to considerable hardship, we find that the *freedom* to enter into a voluntary contractual obligation with a particular capitalist is at the same time the *necessity* to enter into an exploitative relationship with some particular capitalist or other, in order that one and one's dependents do not starve.

### B.    LIBERALISM AND DEMOCRACY

In light of the above, we can now inquire into the relation between the liberal assumptions and democracy. First, insofar as liberal theory assumes the extraction of surplus value as a "natural" foundation of society, there can be no liberal "economic" democracy. But even in merely political terms, during its first two centuries liberal theory was not at all democratic; on the contrary, theorists such as Hobbes, Smith, Malthus and Bentham argued that the greater social good achieved through increased production outweighs any unfortunate effects of the increased inequality of wealth and poverty and the destruction of traditional forms of life. It seemed obvious that only those who own property (both fixed and movable) have a permanent "interest" in society and thus should have the exclusive right to political representation. It was only in the mid-nineteenth century that some liberal theorists such as J. S. Mill and T. H. Green had foresight sufficient to appreciate the potential power of the industrial proletariat and to advocate the democratization of political, but not of economic, life. Their liberal-*democratic* approach, which eventually won widespread acceptance,

called for governmental action to ameliorate the
condition of the proletariat, lest there occur a revolution which would destroy the capitalist order entirely.
This approach led eventually to *welfare-state* liberalism,
in which the basic principles of capitalist production are
left untouched: the government uses its taxation powers
to redistribute a small fraction of the social wealth to
the indigent, while the spheres of production, exchange,
and distribution become increasingly concentrated in
the hands of large-scale enterprises enjoying control over
their respective branches of industry or commerce
("neocapitalism").

Although Popper offers us no concrete picture of his
"open society," it is clear from various remarks that his
ideal is that of a neocapitalist society in which reason is
said to prevail. Since he believes that the state is a
"necessary evil" — which is a classic ideological
obscuration of the reality of the active intervention of
the state *on behalf of* the corporate capitalist class—
what he seeks is a more reasonable society in which conflicts are settled "rationally" by a state open to ideas
and criticism. This means a maximization of input to
those who run the society (owners, managers, politicians,
bureaucrats), who as "rational" individuals will be open
to criticism and will be flexible in their actions. Such a
society would be dynamic by virtue of the "force" of
critical ideas. It would be a free society with equal
opportunities for all to express their opinions, no matter
how diverse or opposed to the status quo, and there
would be institutions by which the "weak" would be
protected from the "strong." But this conception
involves no substantial changes in the theory of liberal
democracy or the neocapitalist social reality, except the
strengthening of the illusion of social harmony through
the appearance of increased discussion and "ration-

ality." For how can one expect that critical ideas which challenged the privileges and power of the owners, managers, etc. would be accepted by these individuals? Why would such a society be any more just than the present version of liberal-democracy, given Popper's admission that there would exist institutions for the protection of the weak from the strong—which means that there would still be "weak" and "strong"—and that these institutions, like everything else, would be under the control of the "strong"? Here Popper naively assumes that good argument alone would prevail, much as it does in the practice of the natural sciences. It must be borne in mind, however, that there is, at least ideally, no power-dimension in the development of scientific theory, but rather that scientists form a *community* with a common interest in the progress of their discipline. Given the antagonistic relations of individuals and classes in any capitalist society, is it not gratuitious to assume that social relations in such a society could ever be analogous to those within the community of scientific researchers?

Political life is a continual struggle for power, either for its continuance or for its transfer. This struggle can be ended only if the power-dimension is eliminated from social life. This, in turn, can be achieved only if three conditions prevail: (1) that all productive property be socially appropriated and subject to the democratic control of the immediate producers within the framework of an economic plan openly and democratically accepted by the majority of the people; (2) that there be no exploitation of some persons by others, which means that there is no extraction of surplus value from one class by another, leaving all economically, politically, and morally equal; and (3) that the citizenry jealously guard its freedom lest, through neglect or otherwise, there arise differentiations of power, giving rise once again to class divisions. Welfare-liberalism, based as it is upon preserving the social inequality of the two most important classes, can never be anything but a limited and formal political democracy, for by definition it denies the majority of the populace access to the economic power which they must have in order to alter their social situation.

## C.   SOCIALISM

By contrast, the socialist conception of man, society, and democracy does not begin from the egoistic man of bourgeois society. Rather, recognizing that for nearly the entire life of the human species the exigencies of survival have dictated cooperative labor and social organization, although of course on a rudimentary level, it regards the egoism and class-division of society, generally prevalent since the founding of the neolithic cultures, as a limitation to be overcome, now that mankind has achieved the material basis of socialism, at least in the developed countries. This "revolution" in human existence requires the utilization of the technical advances of the past two centuries to create a culture —a system of social relations promoting individual development—which surpasses the actual limitations of bourgeois man and is worthy of the vast potential of socialist man. Because socialism inherently involves surpassing the bourgeois limitations on human development (alienation and repression), it is possible only on the basis of a highly developed, automated process of production, in which the advances of the natural sciences are continually transformed into the machines and techniques for overcoming human material want. A socialist society is conceivable only as one of abundance, in which the production of goods and services is measured against the socially-affirmed rational needs of individuals, rather than against the opportunities for private profit in a manipulable market. In economic terms this means creating an economy producing socially-determined use-values rather than exchange-values.

The theoretical framework of critical theory rests on research by Marx into the concrete economic conditions of the particular historical juncture of the capitalist epoch. As such, the Marxist argument is not merely a counterposition to liberalism on the levels of anthropology-axiology and political theory. Given the fact that in the course of developing the materialist interpretation of history, Marx repudiated philosophy and came to regard all merely philosophical analyses as ideological (forms of false consciousness), such a *purely* philosophical consideration of certain premises of the socialist view would be somewhat distorting.[4] All social phenomena exhibit axiological characteristics, and Marxist critical theory, based as it is on the materialist interpretation of history, is value oriented.

From this perspective, the philosophical consideration of axiological problems has a legitimate but subordinate place within critical theory; that it has remained largely undeveloped is probably a vestige of the naturalistic interpretation of Marxism as "scientific socialism" which has generally prevailed since the 1880's. A strong position against this orthodoxy has been taken by Agnes Heller who, following Georg Lukacs, argues:

From the viewpoint of Marxian sociology, it is impossible to empirically derive values. Marx, in fact, did have a fundamental universal value axiom from which all his values and value judgments can be axiologically derived. This ontologically primary and empiricially underivable category is *abundance (Reichtum)*. What is "abundance"? *It is the many-sided unfolding of the essential power of the species.* Thus, we obtain the first value axiom: value is whatever helps the enrichment of the powers of the species: and the second value axiom: the highest value is *the ability of individuals* to appropriate the abundance of the species. [5]

Nonetheless, in their present debate neither Popper nor Marcuse has considered the socialist position in this light. Accordingly, accepting these limitations and restricting ourselves for the time being to the purely philosophical consideration of the political and anthropological-axiological levels, we may note that in place of the conception of the mutual hostility of egoists underlying capitalism and liberalism, Marxists argue from the following propositions, which are themselves derived from the materialist interpretation of history.

(1) The "nature" of man is at all times and places the result of the historical and social circumstances in which men live, and is therefore subject to modification as social relations and conditions themselves change. Such alteration occurs chiefly through the mediation of men themselves, most importantly through labor. Although men are not (at least not yet) the creators of their genetic constitution, it is only to the extent that they create and modify their social and productive relations that they are, collectively, the creators of their own being. Each new generation in its turn modifies the natural environment and the social milieu which it has inherited and which it then passes on to its successors. For the most part, this dialectical process of modification of environment, milieu, and

men themselves has not been a self-conscious one, but rather it has resulted from the aggregation of the unplanned and usually conflicting actions of individuals and groups. Socialists regard the conscious self-creative potentiality of mankind, taken both collectively and individually, and the possibility of replacing a hostile society of egoists with a community of developed individuals, as mankind's distinctively and normatively "human" trait. The concrete actualization of these two potentialities in history is precisely what is meant by socialism.

(2) Thanks in large part to the advances made under capitalism, the current state of productive capacities in the industrialized countries makes it possible to ensure for every person at the very least a sufficiency of those use-values necessary to exist without fear of hunger, poverty, exposure to the elements, lack of medical care, etc. The first social priority is thus that of providing these goods to everyone, regardless of his or her social status.

(3) Each individual has the "right" not to be economically exploited and equally the "responsibility" not to exploit others. It follows that the private ownership of the means of production is incompatible with socialism and that workers themselves must develop ways to regulate production for social needs in such a manner that each producer participates in the production process maximally and in the greatest variety of ways. This would require a major rise in the cultural level and understanding of the members of the working class—indeed, the real appropriation of culture by all members of society instead of by a privileged few whose leisure is gained at the expense of others. At the same time that the production process is to be organized according to the

participation of the producers (workers' self-management), it must also be organized according to the needs of society as a whole and decided upon democratically such that the will of the people actively shapes the planning of production (social self-management). It is at the interface of these two forms of self-management that the institutional organization of a socialist society must emerge and about which it would be pointless at this time to speculate in detail.

(4) It follows that a socialist society will be inherently "political" in all important realms of general concern. It must also be fully democratic, in the sense that all decisions will have to be based upon the widest discussion and participation by all persons concerned. This will of necessity entail the "remaking" of egoists into uncoerced participating members of a community, and will take considerable time to achieve. Without the existence of special economic interests and the power of the privileged, political relations in such a society should be reduced to an effort to identify that course of action which is most in the public interest in any set of circumstances. Obviously the necessary changes in individual outlook upon their society-become-community will be enormous in comparison to the cynicism and egoism currently prevalent.[6] Despite the yawning cultural gap between the actual and the potential, it cannot be overly stressed that *socialism is possible only as democracy* and, equally, that *democracy is actualizable only as socialism.*

(5) Only with the elimination of alienated labor, exploitation, and class-dictatorship, will it become possible for all individuals to partake of the unlimited possibilities of self-development lying both within and without the labor process. That is, in a socialist

society everyone will possess the "right" to the free development of his or her human needs, e.g., self-development, knowledge, sensuality, imagination, creative activity, capacity for communication, solidarity, and beauty.[7] A socialist society would increase personal diversity, as the rigors of a class-determined existence are first reduced and then eliminated. This relates to Marcuse's belief that it will eventually be possible for those who choose to work no more than the socially-necessary minimum (itself to be determined by democratic choice among possible economic plans) to spend most of their time in personal development, interpersonal relations, or enjoyment. Beyond this minimum, work should become a source of enjoyment to those who find their satisfaction in continued, voluntary work, while the lives of all would be enriched by their participation in the numerous aspects of cultural development.[8]

Marcuse makes the interesting suggestion that such a socialist society would arise through a "revolution of disgust" at the injustice, absurdity, and evils of neo-capitalism, now that the poverty of the immediate producers in industrially developed countries is no longer an issue. He sees socialism as entailing the abolition of inane desires fostered through the manipulation of needs, the institution of a rational division of both labor and the social product, and the emancipation of the repressed life-instincts. In other words, he understands socialism as the liberation of people from the exploitative domination of their unconscious motivations, by which their acquisitive, aggressive, and compulsive drives are manipulated and strengthened for the sake of increasing the sale of manufactured gadgets and "industrialized" services, allowing for the free play of the pleasure instinct. His chief point is that, as the productive capacities for conquering men's rational needs exist now, the "revolution of disgust" will take as its touchstone the inhumanity of neocapitalism for the creation of the first normatively "human" society.

Like Popper, however, Marcuse (and socialists generally) gives us only general ideas and not a concrete outline of the society which he seeks.[9] This is a *practical* problem of considerable importance, given the highly effective integration of bourgeois values by the working class, most notably in the United States. On the other hand, the reply that drawing up detailed plans for the society of the future is only to indulge in utopian fantasies which are objectively counter-revolutionary is not unfounded either. But the vagueness of liberals and that of Marxists have different origins. Whereas Marxists have confused the discussion of socialist values with that of preparing utopian blueprints, Popper and other liberal reformers remain vague about their goals because to specify them would be to show their identity with the assumptions underlying the very situation which is in need of reform. Marxists must begin their analysis of socialist values with a critique of the bourgeois anthropological-axiological assumptions, exposing the contrast between the neocapitalist limitations on human development and the possibilities concretely within reach. This is by no means the same thing as drawing up blueprints for utopia; it is rather the working out of the guiding principles of socialist praxis in the anticipated context of advanced economic development proceeding beyond neocapitalism. In this context, praxis would result from the dialectic of the anthropology-axiology of socialism ("Marxian human-ism") and the demands of the concrete political

situation. Even Marxists as committed to the "human-
ist" perspective as the early Lukacs have avoided such
an analysis for purposes of political expediency—i.e.,
they do not wish to raise socialist values over the
possible political needs of the proletariat. Thus, although Lukacs is quite correct in noting that "during
the period of the dictatorship of the proletariat the
nature and the extent of freedom will be determined
by the state of the class struggle, the power of the
enemy, the importance of the threat to the dictatorship, the demands of the classes to be won over, and
by the maturity of the classes allied to and influenced
by the proletariat,"[10] his conclusion that "freedom
cannot represent a value in itself (any more than
socialization)" is no different in principle from that
view which made it appear to the Lenin-Trotsky (and
later Stalin) dictatorship perfectly consistent with
Marxism to ruthlessly destroy the freedom *of the proletariat* when faced with the threat of counterrevolution.[11] Lukacs's statement that "freedom must
serve the rule of the proletariat, not the other way
round,"[12] must not be interpreted to mean that  a
"socialist" bureaucracy can destroy the freedom of the
proletariat precisely in the name of that freedom.

   In view of all this, it should be stated in no un-
certain terms that the "utopian" dimension of socialism in Marcuse's sense, i.e., that mode of thinking
which demands the negation of a present characterized
by alienation and repression in all aspects of life,[13] is
at most half of the Marxian image of the historical
nexus of late capitalism. It was not unintentionally
that Marx excoriated utopianism among socialists and
communists.[14] As Walter Benjamin has put it, the
image of the "liberated grandchildren" is far less
significant for praxis that of the "enslaved ancestors"

or, we might add, the "repressed contemporaries."[15]
After all, *Capital* abounds in studies in exacting detail
of the latter while it ignores the former almost entirely. [16] Of course, the passages on "free time" in Marx's
*Grundrisse* should suffice to refute those Marxists who
would deny the "utopian" dimension in the later Marx
altogether.[17]

## II.  THE LIBERAL AND SOCIALIST
## CONCEPTIONS OF SCIENCE AND PHILOSOPHY

Thus far we have contrasted the views of Marcuse
and Popper in terms of their conceptions of the ideal
society and the anthropological-axiological assumptions
underlying these conceptions. Nonetheless, in arguing
on general philosophical or ideological grounds, we
have sacrificed some concreteness. Thus it might seem
as though the choice between the two "alternative"
conceptions of man, society and democracy, were
simply a matter of *decision*, as though the two
positions are on a par with one another and are ultimately just two alternative metaphysics. As we shall
see below, if the problem is posed in this manner, we
cannot avoid conceding its outcome to Popper, for by
assuming that all choices between ideologies are subjective and idiosyncratic, we would be placing ourselves in the "marketplace of ideas" where nonrational
decisions precede intellectual choices. What must be
shown is that it is not a matter of "choosing" between
liberalism and socialism, but rather that the (relative)
validity of Marxism can be demonstrated on the basis
of two criteria: that of rigor with respect to social and
historical science, and that of adequacy to liberating
praxis in history. We must first show that each posi-

tion represents a different conception of and tradition in science and philosophy—Popper those of naturalism and positivism, and Marcuse those of critical theory and the materialist interpretation of history. Ultimately, the question comes down to the respective conceptions of nature and history and the relations between these and praxis, which now brings us to the second major issue between Popper and Marcuse.

## A.   POPPER'S CONCEPTION OF HISTORY

Popper's approach to history is an exclusively empirical one in which he is at pains to stress history's contingency (against vulgar Marxism, among other opponents) and the impossibility of its democratic control. This is clear in his indictment of the doctrine he calls "historicism," which, along with what he calls "utopianism," is said to be the theoretical basis of totalitarianism. He states:

> I mean by "historicism" an approach to the social sciences which assumes that *historical prediction* is their principal aim, and which assumes that this aim is attainable by discovering the "rhythms" or the "patterns," the "laws" or the "trends" that underlie the evolution of history. . . . And I have not hesitated to construct arguments in its support which have never, to my knowledge, been brought forward by historicists themselves. I hope that, in this way, I have succeeded in building up a position really worth attacking.[18]

It is worth noting that Popper has constructed this

"historicism" — or more accurately, historical naturalism, since it assimilates the study of history to the
natural scientific interest in prediction and control—
from such a variety of doctrines that his critique
reduces to an argument against a straw man.

Be this as it may, his chief argument against the
alleged predictability of history lies in the claim that
history is changed by progress in scientific knowledge,
but that since advances in science are themselves scientifically unpredictable, history itself is scientifically unpredictable. [19] Suffice it to say that non-scientific claims
to the predictability of history are simply dismissed. But
since the course of history is thus held to be unpredictable, Popper's so-called "historicism" is inherently
dogmatic, that is, unscientific; furthermore, it would
follow that there was no history before Copernicus,
Galileo and Newton! Popper claims that when historicism is combined into a ruling ideology with "utopianism," which is also "unscientific" because it is based
upon values and not upon facts, total social control by
the state (totalitarianism) follows. He states:

> The strongest element in the alliance between
> historicism and Utopianism is, undoubtedly, the
> holistic approach which is common to both....
> Both overlook ... the fact that "wholes" in this
> sense can never be the object of scientific inquiry.
> Both parties are dissatisfied with "piecemeal
> tinkering" and "muddling through": they wish to
> adopt more radical methods. ... The control must
> be complete, for in any department of social life
> which is not so controlled, there may lurk the
> dangerous forces that make for unforeseen
> changes.[20]

The difficulties of this argument are many, not the least of which was pointed out by Marcuse when he noted that scientific knowledge only enters into history as *accepted* knowledge, so that the role science plays in historical change must itself be understood in historical terms, rather than history having to be understood in scientific ones.[21] That is, whereas Popper's position implies that scientific ideas affect the course of history directly but unpredictably, they in fact have effect only insofar as science itself forms a constitutive part of the social-historical totality (more strictly, of bourgeois society, given the recent origins of natural science), thus modifying this totality and affecting other social structures within it—production, the state, etc.—only to the extent that the "acceptability" of the scientific ideas in question is mediated by the prevailing state of this totality, which mediation is thus extra-scientific. Progress in many branches of scientific research may have no effect whatsoever on history, or, alternatively, these advances will have an effect to the extent that they are integrated into the social totality, modifying it in turn, which effects may or may not be predictable in social-historical, but not scientific, terms.

This brings us to the heart of the discrepancy between the views of Popper and Marcuse: the question of the status of "totalities"—or, in bourgeois terms, "wholes"—and the capacity of science to treat them rigorously. As we have seen, the most important of Popper's *betes noires* is what he calls "holism," which allegedly is common to historicism and utopianism. This concept represents a confusion on Popper's part between the bourgeois holism of Mannheimian sociology of knowledge and Gestaltism in psychology on the one hand, and the dialectics of socio-historical totalities as in Marx and Lukacs on the other. [22] This holism is but a bourgeois rejection of an equally bourgeois atomism in the attempt to deal with concrete phenomena, especially social and psychological ones. As we shall see below, the bourgeois "whole" differs from the Marxist conception of totality insofar as the former is non-antagonistic. The links between holism, utopianism, historicism and totalitarianism are delineated by Popper as follows:

Holistic or Utopian social engineering, as opposed to piecemeal social engineering ... aims at re-modelling the "whole of society" in accordance with a definite plan or blueprint; it aims at "seizing the key positions" and at extending "the power of the State ... until the State becomes nearly identical with society," and it aims, furthermore, at controlling from these "key positions" the historical forces that mould the future of the developing society: either by arresting this develop-ment, or else by foreseeing its course and adjusting society to it.[23]

Given this relation, Popper's case against historicism rests upon the connection between the assumed pre-dictability of historical events and the possibility of that control over them which, Popper assumes, implies a totalitarian state. For history to be determined, human actions must exhibit a completely thinglike character, just as classical mechanics requires its objects to have no "internal" motion but to move entirely in accord with external forces. On the other hand, the classical argu-ment for the indeterminism of history is that of the alleged existence of human "free will," which supposedly ensures that individuals can and do act with-out external causes (voluntarism). Obviously, only on the first of these views would history be predictable, and so Popper's "historicists" must be determinists, since they assume history is predictable. Yet Popper's "totalitarians" are assumed to control history completely (at least within a given society), so they need to be extreme voluntarists, as Stalin and Hitler indeed were. Thus, despite Popper's desire to identify them, the "historicists" and the "totalitarians" hold contradictory conceptions of history.

## B.   THE MARXIAN CONCEPTION OF HISTORY

For Marxism, the whole argument over predictability is entirely beside the point. Although the vulgar Marxists of the Second International, and the Bolsheviks, were determinists in their philosophy of history,[24] there is no justification in Marxian socialism for such determinism, or for voluntarism. In fact, the interrelated Marxian conceptions of man, praxis, and history all imply in the strongest terms the indeterminability of historical events. This indeterminability is not voluntaristic but rather is *ambiguous*, as long as societal life is not organized socialistically. This will be the case as long as Marx's observation holds, viz., that "men make their own history, but they do not make it just as they please; they do not make it under circumstances chosen by themselves, but under circumstances directly encountered, given and transmitted from the past. The tradition of all the dead generations weighs like a nightmare on the brain of the living."[25] This will be the case as long as men are still (1) acting individualistically, without social control over social production, and (2) under the domination of the inherited inadequacy of "tradition"—that is, scarcity. On the contrary, realized "Communism" for Marx is precisely the overcoming of these two conditions; and it is for this reason that he considers it to be the *telos* of history. As he formulated this point in 1844,

> Communism is the positive abolition of private property, of human self-alienation, and thus the real appropriation of human nature through and for man. It is . . . a complete and conscious return [of man to himself] which assimilates all the wealth of previous development . . . . It is the definitive resolution of the antagonism between man and nature, and between man and man. . . . It is the solution to the riddle of history and knows itself to be this solution.[26]

Only at this stage of social and economic development will men's freedom be grounded in a democratic "voluntarism" involving all members of society and differing from previous voluntarisms by supporting their freedom of self-development and not their enslavement to the totalitarian state. Prior to such a stage, however, men and their social relations will continue to exhibit thinglike (objectlike) characteristics in some important respects. Individuals will often fail to behave as free agents but rather will exhibit such lawlike behavior as makes possible a limited form of approximate historical prediction. But this predictability must be understood as a symptom of that reification of individuals and their social relations which is a historical consequence of class-dominated societies. Even so, human action, and hence history, is always ambiguous because no matter how overwhelming the alienation of this reification might seem, men are always potentially and in part actually free beings, capable of negating their reified social milieu, of modifying it, or even destroying it and

creating a new one through revolutionary praxis. To this
extent, even in a controlled totalitarian system such as
that of Stalinism, social relations never admit the strict
and total determinism (and predictability) of natural
events. Men are always subjects, although prior to the
full development of socialism they are always alienated
ones; in the terminology of the early Lukacs, they are
the "identical subject-objects" of history, who possess
the potentiality of reappropriating their individual and
collective subjectivity, i.e., their freedom. It should be
noted that Lukacs reserves the term "identical subject-
object of history" for the proletariat, and does not
apply it to "mankind" at large, because at this historical
juncture only the proletariat is a class which is almost
entirely an object and which can also transcend this
objectivity by creating a new social totality through
revolutionary praxis. [27] Similarly, Maurice Merleau-
Ponty writes:

> Even in a Marxist perspective effective history
> follows its internal logic to the very end only if
> men become aware of it, understand it in the
> Marxist sense, and complete the movement which
> is [only] roughly indicated in things. The historian
> who writes the history of 1917 cannot, even if he
> is a Marxist, pretend that the revolution was
> predestined; he must [on the contrary] show it
> was possible—even probable—but not prefabri-
> cated. The course of universal history is
> not determined even for him: socialism will come,
> but who knows when or by what paths? [28]

Thus, Marxists do not agree with Popper that history
is simply contingent, although they know it to be
subject to the vicissitudes, for the most part beyond

anyone's control, of the actions of individuals and groups. They further agree that predictability in detail is precluded, for they are *not* historicists as Popper has defined the terms. That is,

> Marxism . . . recognizes that nothing in history is absolutely contingent, that historical facts . . . form an intelligible system and present a rational development. But the characteristic thing about Marxism . . . is its admission that . . . the final synthesis is not necessitated but depends upon a revolutionary act whose certainty is not guaranteed by any divine decree nor by any metaphysical structure of the world . . . . It is therefore characteristic of Marxism to admit that history is both logical and contingent, that nothing is absolutely fortuitous but also that nothing is absolutely necessary—which is what we meant . . . when we said that there are dialectical facts. [29]

Yet, given the ambiguity of history, it is possible and indeed necessary for praxis to undertake the scientific project of analyzing the forces and structures present in any historical nexus in order to discover the tendencies which are present, as in Merleau-Ponty's affirmation that "socialism will come, but who knows when or by what paths." The classical analysis demonstrating this is, of course, that of Marx in *Capital*. This analysis does not assume that history is determined by causal laws as discovered by natural science, but it does indicate the probable direction of historical movement given certain assumptions about the probable behavior of individuals who make up historically-significant social groups: for example, the behavior of individual capitalists at various stages of the business cycle, behavior which invariably leads to the repetition of the cycle, despite their own wishes. This gives us a glimpse, although only a brief one at this stage of the argument, at the differences between the naturalistic and the Marxian conceptions of the nature and functions of social science (in this case history), conceptions which we shall see underlie the entire problematic of the liberal and socialist *Weltanschauungen*.

## C.   SCIENTIFIC NATURALISM

Popper, who rejects determinism in history, none-theless assumes it for the study of nature, since his model of science is that of the natural sciences—most importantly physics, a model which has been the paradigm of natural science since the seventeenth century. It was in physics that Galileo and Newton established for the first time the efficacy of what Popper was later to call the "hypothetical-deductive method." Yet ironically, insofar as Popper would have the social sciences modeled on the natural sciences, he contradictorily introduces a deterministic model into the study, and thus into the desired "engineering" of society, a move which places him in the camp of those who would reduce people to things and manipulate their reified social relations.

To appreciate the roots of this irony, we must recognize that the naturalism of classical physics is essentially bourgeois, and that it shares with the market economy and other liberal presuppositions a common foundation in the basic assumption of a reified world. Furthermore, when the natural sciences are assumed to be the only fitting paradigms of the

social sciences (or "sciences of man") their own underlying bourgeois foundations are inevitably hidden. This
results in turn in the complicity of the social sciences
in the bourgeois (today neocapitalist) order such that
significant structural change (liberation) is banished
from the horizon of these sciences and from the
"piecemeal social engineering" of the "open society"
which is supposed to be based upon them.

The basic achievement of Galileo in founding the
methodology of the natural sciences was the formula-
tion and successful demonstration of a paradigm of a
systematic rational knowledge of nature, newly
defined by him as *objective nature*, which would lead
eventually to a system of demonstrable, i.e., deductive,
propositions characterizing the law-governed determined interactions of pure bodies. [30] Such an abstract,
objective nature is obviously not the "nature" of our
everyday experience. The "nature" we meet when we
walk through a forest, look up at the stars, or notice
animals or plants, is not "objective" but rather a
compound of instinctual, practical, religious, aesthetic
and other such meanings. Mathematics is necessary to
natural science in order to underpin that process of
abstraction from these meanings which enables the
scientist to speak of a purely objective nature
governed by laws. The ultimate goal of the Galilean
revolution is the conception of everything that exists
as a body or a complex of bodies, and of all phenomena as events resulting from the interactions of
bodies. The goal of classical natural science and the
accompanying rationalist philosophy was thus a systematic *episteme* of objective nature, a program that
would overcome the ambiguity of the experienced
world, now to be characterized with the epithet "subjective." [31] With widespread acceptance by the literate

public of this subjective-objective distinction, the fact that science originates in an explicit abstraction from pre-scientific experience, recognized clearly by Galileo but gradually forgotten as science became increasingly a matter of intellectual technique, lost its strangeness and became obscured. This made it possible for the naive ontology of natural objects (Galileo's "pure bodies") to become widely accepted by philosophers by the eighteenth century (hence Kant's "Copernican revolution" in epistemology) and subsequently by the general public. It is worth noting in passing that classical modern philosophy, i.e., rationalism, originated with Descartes and Hobbes, who saw its task to be the grounding of natural science in indubitable "first truths" (later, Kant's "transcendental logic"), from which ensuing propositions concerning objective nature would derive their validity. Only with Hume's skepticism did there arise the positivist repudiation of the ideal of a deductive system of science originating in metaphysics, with the result that a modern Humean such as Popper could state that science is not a system of truths but only one of tentative hypotheses.

Hence Popper states, correctly, that the natural sciences "do not consist of positive or certain knowledge," but he draws from this the false conclusion that there is "no positive, certain knowledge, there is but hypothetical knowledge." He objects to the Marxists because "they think they know a great deal," which is to say that they are dogmatic; but his own skepticism reduces to nihilism, since, if science cannot give us certain knowledge (*episteme*) but only hypotheses, it does not follow that there is no such possible *episteme* unless one gratuitously identifies all knowledge with scientific knowledge. On the contrary, the phenomenological school of philosophy has amply demonstrated that all forms of conceptualization are grounded in pre-predicative experience, the "knowledge" of which cannot be based upon the conceptualized paradigm of the natural sciences. This is the case because the pre-scientific experiences of meaning which were occluded with the expansion of natural scientific objectivism are in principle prior to, and untouched by, this process of objectification. [32] Popper's skepticism amounts to the dogmatic and false denial that there can be any knowledge other than natural scientific knowledge, and the correct claim that scientific knowledge itself is hypothetical and not epistemic. This attitude has the effect of precluding investigation of the human realm, the realm of experienced meanings including specifically socialized ones, in any way other than by the misplaced reduction of experience to natural events and the interaction of bodies. Thus, Popper's denial that he is a positivist is ridiculous. By narrowly defining positivism as teaching "Stay with what is perceived," Popper identifies positivism with the limited perspective of the Vienna Circle, which in general sees science as inductively empirical. Popper's chief contribution is to have seen and demonstrated that science is not inductive at all, but deductive. Nonetheless, this is not sufficient to spare him from the charge of being a positivist: his positivism consists precisely in the claim that "above all there is scientific progress." This is pure positivism in the Comtean tradition, the uncritical faith in the transformative powers of natural science and the uncritical acceptance of the obfuscation of its own bourgeois "metaphysical" presuppositions. Furthermore, as we shall see, the realm of social significations is characterized by the presence of *totalities*, the parts of which are united by func-

tional and dialectical relations, rather than merely by
bodies and their aggregations, as well as by *negativities*. With this vast field open for investigation, dialectically and phenomenologically, there is no reason
to concede to Popper that *episteme* is impossible. This
point is central to Marxism for, to cite Merleau-
Ponty again,

> It is precisely this idea, that nothing can be
> isolated in the total context of history, which lies
> at the heart of Marxism, with, in addition, the
> idea that because of their greater generality
> economic phenomena make a greater contribution
> to historical discourse—not that they explain
> everything that happens but that no progress can
> be made in the cultural order, no historical step
> can be taken unless the economy . . . is organized
> in a certain way. [33]

In fact, Popper's skeptical imputation of a latent
dogmatism to Marxism reflects the positivist dogma
that there is no "truth" in politics, that all values
are subjective (i.e. idiosyncratic and indemonstrable).
It follows that any claim to criticize bourgeois institutions and values would a priori be "unscientific"
because science allegedly deals only with facts and not
with values. Needless to say, Marxism denies the
concreteness of this distinction, and relegates it to the
realm of positivist abstraction because there are no
social phenomena which are not both factual and
normative. Natural science deals with projected
objectivities, which are idealizations, rather than with
nature as it is concretely experienced even by the
scientist. The reader should note Hegel's remark concerning scientific observation, that "consciousness

'observes,' i.e., reason wants to find and to have itself in the form of [an] existent object, to *be* in [the] concrete sensuously-present form. [But] consciousness thus observing believes [*meint*] and, indeed, says that it wants to discover not itself, but, on the contrary, the inner being [i.e., the laws] of things qua things."[34]

The proper Marxist response to positivist nihilism masquerading as *the* philosophy of science, and its debasing of all criticism of positive social facts as being "merely subjective" or "emotive" consists in actually working out the theory of the praxis, especially in labor, and thereby the theory of society, nature and history, so as to demonstrate the existence of the "normative" *in* the phenomenal by studying social-historical phenomena in their concreteness. That is, Marxism denies the reification of objective facts, and the subjectivization of values. This distinction is based upon destroying the context of concrete phenomena, as Lukacs notes when he states that "the 'pure' facts of the natural sciences arise when a phenomenon of the real world is placed (in thought or reality) into an environment where its laws can be inspected without outside interference. This process is reinforced by reducing phenomena to their purely quantitative essence."[35] In contrast to this, the occluded meaning of Galilean science as the objectification of Being, with its parallels in Descartes's metaphysics and Hobbes's psychology and social theory, is by no means accidentally related to the objectification or reification of the social relations and consciousness characteristic of the bourgeois society which was forming in the womb of feudalism contemporaneously with the first successes of natural science.

As Marx has shown, capitalism arose as the fedual

economy was being transformed into a system of production based exclusively upon commodity production, and especially on the reduction of the laborer to the commodity "labor-power." Now, a commodity is nothing but an *economic object*, the crystallization of living labor standing over against its producers and dominating them, i.e., turning them into *its* objects. [36] The labor process in capitalism is nothing but the reified activity of the laborer as an object (the commodity labor-power) upon other objects (raw materials, tools, etc.), all of which are the property of the capitalist. From the latter's viewpoint, the labor process is simply the consumption of all these commodities which he has purchased in order to produce surplus value, "a process between *things* ... that have become his property." [37] The laborer can only regain his subjectivity (and still an alienated one at that) *outside* the labor process, in his free time and when he "freely" seeks another labor contract with another capitalist. Because the capitalist labor process is nothing but the interaction of objects for private profit, it is an atomizing process: it is based on the uncoordinated actions of individuals in total economic competition with one another. There is no functioning interest in the economic whole, the local, regional, national and international production—exchange—distribution—consumption process, but only the antagonistic interplay of isolated economic "atoms." As a functional part of bourgeois society as a totality, nascent science shared in the atomism and objectivism of this society and its implicit view of the world, as Popper has grasped in noting that " 'wholes' ... can never be the object of [naturalistic] scientific inquiry." [38]

Thus we have Popper's testimony to the atomism, as well as Galileo's to the objectivism, of natural science, both of which are salient characteristics of nascent bourgeois society. In contrast, Marxism denies that science must be objectivistic and atomistic; instead, regarding *social* science, these attributes only ideologize it. As Merleau-Ponty has put it, "sociology cannot recognize any permanent elements in the different wholes into which they are integrated [i.e., the rejection of the constancy-hypothesis, already developed by the Gestalt psychologists], no facts external to one another, but, in the case of each society, should recognize a totality where phenomena give mutual expression to each other and reveal the same basic theme."[39]

We can now see why Popper's attempt to maximize natural scientific rationality in neocapitalist social relations represents the application of a highly refined bourgeois metaphysics (which Popper would deny, since it is buried beneath the postivist self-conception of science) as well as an equally refined method to an advanced state of bourgeois social development. Thus, the cure and the symptoms are but different manifestations of the same malady. We can now also see that the reason Popper does not give any concrete picture of the "open society" and the role to be played therein by scientific "reason" is that it would not differ in any essentials from the contemporary western neocapitalist democracies. The formalism of the "open society," which is based on the ideological notion of the "marketplace of ideas" and which possesses all the "freedom" of the capitalist marketplace, follows directly from Popper's theory of science, which in turn follows from his acceptance of the positivist separation of fact and value. This separation is the basis of his argument against the "Platonism" which he detects with some justification in Hegel (and in vulgar Marxism, we should add) but which is, despite Popper's assertions, not present in Marx. [40] Popper's critique of Plato is motivated by the goal of refuting all claims that there might be knowledge of political values; yet Popper speaks in a loose manner of the "value" of every human being, a concept which can never be justified on the basis of his theory of science. Thus, when he speaks of the "moral superiority" of rationalism—by which he means the rejection of every claim to intellectual authority—and of the non-totalitarian attitude which allegedly follows from this rationalism, we must note that this skepticism merely masks the irrational authority of liberalism, from which point of view all political values are equally unverifiable.

This irrationalism is shown up by the telling points made below by the interviewer: (1) that the "social evils" which Popper wishes to see remedied are themselves values albeit negative ones (or better, that they are phenomena, in that "facts" and "values" have no existence except in the analysis of the positivist) and therefore on his own grounds Popper could never have knowledge of them upon which to base piecemeal reform; and (2) that the whole idea of the "open society" is based upon the *belief* in the moral superiority of naturalistic reason, which belief must itself be irrational or nonrational and whose "moral superiority," itself a value, could never be demonstrated "scientifically."

As Bacon phrased it at the dawn of the seventeenth century scientific revolution, "Knowledge is power"—by which we must understand power over both nature and men. As such, the political use of what Popper calls "critical" scientific reason would uncritically overlook the fundamental flaws of the contemporary neocapitalist western democracies, although it might streamline the prevailing system by making things more efficient. "Critical" discussions would be solely about choosing the most efficient means, and the only significant participants would be those who have a monopoly on knowledge of means, *viz.*, the technicians and managers, and those who have already established the ends, *viz.*, the owners, politicians and bureaucrats. Popper's "open society" would in fact be the St.-Simonian autocracy of the owners and the men of science.

## D.  CRITICAL THEORY

But the problem of the homology of science and bourgeois society as a totality becomes even more acute in the *social* sciences, which deal in large measure with the problems of this very society. With respect to political economy, it is here that Marx argued that a bourgeois social science could be nothing but an obfuscation of the status quo of capitalism because of its blindness to its own theoretical foundations in its acceptance of capitalism. Marx differentiated himself from the political economists by understanding these foundations in political and historical rather than in natural terms. He saw the goal of his theoretical work as changing political economy into a critical social science, a critique of the economic presuppositions of capitalism which was to be accomplished by criticizing classical political economy and demonstrating the historical origins and fate of capitalism. Such a critical economic science would, then, be the theoretical framework of a thoroughly democratic and socialist society in which nothing would be beyond discussion and criticism; among other things, this science would demonstrate the necessity of workers' and social self-management in such a society. The same would be true of all praxis leading up to the transition to socialism, which must be understood within the framework of a critical theory that anticipates it while being nourished by present social-historical realities. For Max Horkheimer, critical theory "confronts history with that possibility which is always concretely visible within it." [41] Similarly, for Marx

> the construction of the future and its completion for all times is not our task, what we have to accomplish ... is all the more clear: *relentless criticism of all existing conditions*, relentless in the sense that the criticism is not afraid of its findings and just as little afraid of the conflict with the powers-that-be. [42]

Insofar as classical political economy failed to question the foundations of capitalism as to its anthropological-axiological assumptions and its historical limitations, it was for Marx unworthy of the name "science." Marxian critical social science, whose paradigm is the critique of political economy, is distinguished from its bourgeois counterpart in that it seeks to provide, by its radical anatomy of capitalism as the exploitation of alienated labor, the theoretical knowledge needed to transform that social system by revolutionary praxis. Positivist social science, on the other hand, accepts the existence of capitalism as "natural" in order to reduce it to facts for analysis and in order to assist the capitalists by advising them how to make the system function more efficiently. The philosophical or anthropological-axiological basis of Marx's critique of classical political economy is his conception of the authentic potentialities of human existence in an advanced industrial society, and of the alienation of bourgeois man (proletarian and capitalist alike), which he had worked out in his manuscripts of 1844. The metaphilosophical basis of this critique is the materialist interpretation of history, in which all technical economic questions are addressed within the context of bourgeois society as a developing self-contradictory historical totality.

To appreciate fully the contrast between Marxian and naturalistic social science we must recall the crucial role played in the former by the concept of totality and its repudiation by naturalistic science as represented by Popper. As Lukacs has noted, Marx's statement that " 'the relations of production of every society form a whole' is the methodological point of departure and the key to the *historical* understanding of social relations." [43] The Marxist dialectic, far from being laws of nature as Engels had maintained, [44] is rather an approach to the study of historical phenomena which stresses the antagonistic character of social totalities and the negativities inherent in them.

> It is not the primacy of economic motives in historical explanation that constitutes the decisive difference between Marxian and bourgeois thought, but the point of view of totality. . . . Proletarian science is revolutionary not just by virtue of its revolutionary ideas which it opposes to bourgeois society, but above all because of its method. *The primacy of the category of totality is the bearer of the principle of revolution in science.* [45]

The "facts" of positivist social science, which are considered as given ("positively") and in mutual isolation
are themselves products of the social system.

> Thus, when "science" maintains that the manner
> in which data immediately present themselves is
> an adequate foundation of scientific conceptualiza-
> tion and that the actual form of these data is
> the appropriate starting point for the formation
> of scientific concepts, it thereby takes its stand
> simply and dogmatically on the basis of capitalist
> society. It uncritically accepts the nature of the
> object as it is given and the laws of that society
> as the unalterable foundation of "science." [46]

Instead, these "facts" must be understood in terms of
their historical origins and relations rather than as
immediately given; that is, they must be examined
historically and dialectically. This in turn means that
the facts must be understood in terms of an antagonistic totality, as capitalism was analyzed by Marx,
for these "contradictions" belong to the very nature
of social reality. Our understanding of social phenomena is a matter of understanding their function in
terms of their place in the social-historical *process*.

On the other hand, bourgeois society wants to
understand its existence as harmonious and its values
as eternal. This is the function of bourgeois social
science. When the ideal of scientific knowledge is
applied to nature it validly furthers our knowledge,
even if hypothetical. But when it is applied to society
this ideal becomes an ideological weapon of the bourgeoisie. Bourgeois social science "must think of
capitalism as being predestined to eternal survival by
the eternal laws of nature and reason. Conversely, con-

tradictions that cannot be ignored must be shown to be purely surface phenomena." [47] Specifically, the stress on "objectivity" in economics conceals the fact that economic categories are reified forms of the relations of capitalist production. The economic system appears as a mechanism for the production of "goods" and "services" according to the "law" of supply and demand, but what is overlooked is that these economic categories represent nothing other than the exploitation of labor and alienated and dehumanized social relations. Thus, the Marxist critique of political economy is not merely a disagreement among economists about economic problems, but an explicit critique of the classical economists' acceptance of the capitalist system of production as "natural" and an implicit critique of the application of natural scientific methodology to social-historical reality. We may note in passing that Marx's critique applies *mutatis mutandis* to neoclassical, marginalist, and Keynesian economics as well.

Far from being caught in the positivist dichotomy of values and facts, which thinks of political presuppositions as biasing one's scientific analyses—as even the leading Marxist economists of the Second International believed—Marx's critical approach to the economic and other phenomena of bourgeois society enabled him as a revolutionary to mediate his theory with emancipatory praxis. This revolutionary capacity in Marx's theory raises for us the central question of the philosophy of the social sciences: What is the *interest* which guides their cognitive inquiry? [48] In the case of the natural sciences, the guiding interest is that of *control* over nature. The social sciences, insofar as they remain naturalistic, have as their own interest the working out of this concern for control in terms of their study of social relations. A critical social science, on the other hand, has as its guiding interest the *emancipation* of men from dehumanizing social relations. As such, the critical social sciences have a clearly defined relation to praxis which is lacking in the positivist naturalist social sciences, whose claims to "objectivity" conceal their roots in, and uncritically accept, the capitalist totality.

### E.  UNIQUE PROBLEMS OF SOCIAL SCIENCE

The problem of interest is acute in the social sciences precisely because the observer does not study an abstract object-world, but rather meaning-structures, which do not admit of reduction to the form of objective laws as do natural phenomena. Despite their reification in bourgeois society, human agents are conscious, value-oriented beings who seek to achieve various goals through their actions. Furthermore, the value system that is studied by the social scientist is by and large a part of his own life history, sedimented in the meaning-structure of his experience and his *Weltanschauung*. Thus either (1) he is a part of what he investigates (or better, it is a part of him) and cannot exclude his affections even in cognitive operations as basic as the organization of data, or (2) he is as objective as possible and thus makes himself into an outsider who is unaffected by the object of his study, in which case he cannot experience the social meaning-structure he is investigating as it is experienced by members of the social system under investigation; that is, his knowledge remains mediated by his techniques. In the first case there is necessarily a loss of objectivity but perhaps a compensating increase in insight, whereas in the second there is the loss of the intuitive knowledge which makes the members of the society under investigation able to grasp the meaning-structures in question by living through them. "The knowledge of the real ... nature of a phenomenon, the knowledge of its historical character and the knowledge of its actual function in the totality of society, form ... a single, individual act of cognition. The unity is shattered by the pseudo-scientific method." [49]

But a critical, non-positivist social science must be more than the intuitions of individual researchers; it must be based upon a dialectical conception of reason which guides it both methodologically and axiologically. We can distinguish two methods of scientific investigation which have had success in their respective domains: (1) that of causal explanation (*Erklärung*) in the natural sciences and (2) that of interpretation (*Verstehen* or *Hermeneutik*) in the humanities. The social sciences are problematical because of the ambiguity of social forms, which are neither entirely law-determined nor the expressions of creative spirit. Insofar as human action is often unfree, and social relations often reified, natural scientific methodology plays a legitimate, if limited, role in the sciences of man. Indeed there are aspects of social life, especially in a capitalist society, which show thinglike characteristics and lawlike regularity. But, on the other hand, insofar as men are goal-oriented, evaluating, creative beings, social science must appropriate the method of *Verstehen* in its investigation of the meaning-structures of men's social world(s). A dialectical social science is one which, through its logic and its interpretation of history, mediates the apparent contradiction between these two methods as it attempts to understand a social system as a totality. Rather than being merely

an application of natural science to the domain of
social "facts," such a critical social science has available to it two modes of emancipation: the individual
one of psychological therapy and the collective one of
political activity. In both modes, critical social science
mediates theory and emancipatory praxis. The
function of the critical social scientist is thus to aid in
the process of overcoming that dehumanization of
individuals and of social relations which characterizes
neocapitalist society, since his theoretical research into
the grounds of this dehumanization is inherently
related to emancipatory praxis.

The interviewer's question below to Marcuse concerning the criteria necessary to justify the "correctness" of the new society indicates the difference
between *critical theory* and *utopian thinking*. In the
latter case, the values sought for the new society are
indemonstrable precisely because a utopian value-
system is unrelated to existing historical conditions and
so is said to be valid for all time. But critical theory
recognizes that, just as facts and values are not distinct
in reality, although every social phenomenon *may* be
reduced to a "fact" and a "value" upon analysis, so
too it recognizes that social phenomena are not static
but are always changing toward the horizon of the
future, as the potentialities of societies continue to
change. Critical theory criticizes irrational social
phenomena to the extent that they are dehumanizing
and analyzes their potential for transformation. In so
doing, it can point to various historical possibilities in
any given situation. The critical theorist can justify
one or more of these possibilities in terms of his
philosophical anthropology and the materialist interpretation of history, which we have seen to be axiological in part. But only the actual movement of

history will decide among the possibilities specified by the theorist, or create new ones he had not anticipated. Thus, the specific role of the theorist is that of criticizing the irrational and clarifying the alternatives, not that of leading revolutions or of building new societies. As Marx observed,

> we do not face the world in doctrinaire fashion with a new principle, declaring, "Here is truth, kneel here!" We develop new principles for the world out of the principles of the world. We do not tell the world, "Cease your struggles, they are stupid; we want to give you the true watchword of the struggle." We merely show the world why it actually struggles; and the awareness of this is something that the world *must* acquire even if it does not want to.[50]

## III. SCIENCE AND POLITICAL PRAXIS

This brings us to our third major issue: that of the respective ways of attaining the two contrasting goals of Marcuse and Popper. Popper gives us no answer to the question as to how the "open society" can be realized, except the claim that it will be by "piecemeal social engineering" and the pious hope that "reason," by which is meant that natural, scientific, instrumental reason which we now know to be uncritical in the neocapitalist social context, may prevail. Granting that there is a great deal of such "rational" criticism generated from all levels of our society, we must still ask why those who possess power would be interested in following this criticism if it is in any way prejudicial to their interests. Furthermore, it seems

obvious that any criticism which radically questions
the foundations of our society will find no favor
among the owners and social "engineers." What
Popper completely ignores is that in a class society
political life revolves around the question of *power*; it
may *incidentally* include such things as discussion,
rights, elections, and the like, but those who already
possess social power have to be coerced into acting
upon any criticism which does not support their
interests, no matter how socially constructive that
criticism might be. But this brings us immediately to
the matter of political violence, by which is meant
coercion of all degrees and types, which Popper is
anxious to avoid.

If we were to accept the ends suggested by Popper,
the only means of bringing about the "piecemeal
social engineering" of which he speaks are proscribed
by him. It is this illusion that reform is possible
without entering into political struggle, that it can be
achieved solely by the force of disinterested argument
among men and women of good will, which reveals
the glaringly ideological nature of Popper's "open
society." Such a society is impossible to actualize
within the limits set by Popper himself, and, even if it
could be achieved, it would gain us nothing in terms
of human emancipation. It would be necessary that all
reforms be indeed in the interest of the ruling class for
them to undertake the "engineering" necessary to
bring them about. Nevertheless, in *The Poverty of
Historicism*, after correctly arguing that the *utopian*
social engineer would have to be vested with almost
dictatorial powers in order to be able to carry out his
program, Popper observes,

I do not believe that any corresponding criticism

of the piecemeal method can be offered. This method can be used ... to search for, and fight against, the greatest and most urgent evils of society, rather than to seek, and to fight for, some ultimate good. ... But a systematic fight against definite wrongs, against concrete forms of injustice and exploitation, and avoidable suffering such as poverty or unemployment, is a very different thing from the attempt to realize a distant ideal blueprint of society. ... There is no inherent reason why this method should lead to an accumulation of power, and to the suppression of criticism. [51]

As we have seen, even "piecemeal" social engineering is social engineering within a class society; the control over that society may be delegated to the social engineers, but it will nonetheless remain vested in the hands of the owners and bureaucrats. The accumulation of power would in fact *increase* in such a society, since the engineering would begin on the basis of power already accumulated by the monopolists and oligopolists who own and control the means of production. As outlined above, they would expect their interests to be served by any proposed social "reforms." It is evident from this passage that Popper treats "concrete forms of injustice or exploitation" as positive facts without considering their roots in a capitalist system of production common to both the contemporary reality and Popper's proposed "open society." There are, for Popper, only the two alternatives of dictatorial utopian planning and "open" piecemeal reform. His point that all dictatorships, whether of the left or the right, are the same is valid *only* if the starting point is that of a democracy, although an imperfect one, such as in the contemporary western democracies. Although it is an enormous problem which cannot be resolved here, it is incumbent upon socialists to address themselves to the question of the organization of the revolutionary movement and of post-revolutionary institutions in order to guard against the recrudescence of dictatorial tendencies in future socialist society. It should be obvious that the Soviet experience with "democratic centralism" in Party and State has been a political as well as a human disaster. On the other hand, the Chinese experience, despite the ever-present danger of authoritarian bureaucracy, appears thus far to have avoided sinking into an irreversible bureaucratic centralism. Regardless of this, however, the point to be made here is that neither side of Popper's dichotomy leads to human emancipation. Socialism is no utopia; as Marx once said, the forced changing of social circumstances by a few individuals possessing the Truth (Popper's utopian engineering, either with or without the democratic facade) "must divide society into two parts, one of which is superior to the other."[52] But the question of means admits of at least three, not just two, alternative answers. The way out of the dilemma, which will lead to fundamental structural change in the direction of emancipation, is through the concerted action of the people, leading themselves and establishing a democratic socialism. This is neither "utopian" dictatorship nor mere piecemeal reform.

The goal of the truly open society—that is, socialist society—can be achieved, if at all, only through a protracted struggle. As long as the United States remains the bastion of world neocapitalism, the world will remain the scene of continued conflict as various peoples struggle to free themselves from foreign economic domination. Given their economic underdevelopment, this is by no means equivalent to the immediate struggle for human emancipation, but is merely one condition for its eventual attainment. At the same time, any domestic manifestation of the struggle for fundamental social change will meet with repression, the subtler the better from the government's point of view.[53]

Popper would have us believe that progress in our ideas and the application of science to social problems can replace violent revolutions. But there has never been a non-violent social revolution. His positivist faith in the intrinsic relation of scientific progress to the happiness of mankind ignores the fact that politics is never "disinterested" as long as society is divided along class lines, any more than is science. Popper also refers to the distinction between a peaceful and violent overthrow, and alleges that Marxists have never adequately dealt with this ambiguity. In a certain sense he is right, for Marxists do not consider the question of violence to be fundamental; what is fundamental is emancipation, not the means necessary to achieve it.[54] As noted above, however, there are, nonetheless, certain guidelines which define the emancipatory nature of the political struggle which must not be violated. The only realistic reply to Popper on this point is that, hopefully, given a transition from neocapitalism to socialism, only that amount of force will be used which is *absolutely necessary*, and no more. But we can be sure that *at least* as much force as the bourgeoisie presently uses to defend its privileges will have to be used against it, and that in the last analysis this is what will decide the general level of violence.

We know as well that the bourgeoisies of numerous countries have already shown themselves willing to embrace fascism when they have considered it necessary. Because the ruling class already possesses a near-monopoly on the means of force, it is obviously wise for revolutionaries to avoid the use of violence for some time.

They will have to develop means of struggle other than direct, violent confrontation, such as mass economic action, including strikes and boycotts, election campaigns, legal actions directed against the corporations and the government, and the so-called infiltration of important social institutions. The political struggles that have occurred in the past decade give some ground for hope that these seeds will fall on fertile ground. The antiwar movement demonstrated that widespread and sustained popular opposition to the government can prevent it from carrying out its aims with impunity. In the process, millions of Americans had their eyes opened for the first time to the brutality "normally" perpetrated in their name, and we may well suspect that despite the current political lull the political consciousness of the people will never be quite the same. But the political activity of the 1960's failed to produce a permanent mass radical opposition, especially a radical working class one, as dissent was diffused by the liberal-reformist candidacies of McCarthy, Kennedy, and McGovern, and by the government's use of force, as at Kent State. True, the political consciousness of the exploited minorities was raised considerably. But in terms of political power, these groups can at best only disrupt the system; they do not have sufficient power to bring it to a standstill. It is not unrealistic to envision the wholesale repression of these groups should they begin to pose a serious threat to the established order. Similarly, the student movement, which as of this writing has been largely dissipated, simply cannot wield the power necessary to shake the system to its foundations. This is true despite the fact that, in the long run, the dissemination of critical ideas among future generations is of paramount importance for breaking the syndrome of the automatic conformity of the younger generation to the consumer society. The women's movement, for its part, possesses the potential of challenging the foundations of a social system which exploits both the men who are forced into alienated labor and the women who are either exploited in the labor force or excluded from it entirely by prejudice. Still, the economic and political power of the political segment of the women's movement is as yet quite limited. The only real possibility of bringing neocapitalist society to a standstill remains with the workers as workers rather than fragmented as women or minority groups. It is only with the formation of a mass socialist workers' movement which will not hesitate to act as a radical political force that there is any significant possibility of asserting the power necessary to bring about the collapse of the bourgeois state — or, for that matter, significant social reform. Only the working class has the potential to create a socialist society, since the fundamental problem to be overcome in the transition to socialism is precisely the alienation of labor.

It is essential however, that the transition to socialism occur from below and that production be organized from below at all levels, for no party, bureaucracy, or state can replace the free association of the people. Only in this way can socialism fulfill all that it promises. It follows that a radical labor movement is the single most important condition necessary, although by itself not sufficient for the growth of a broad socialist movement. The current conditions and loyalties of the leadership of the American working class should give sufficient indication of how far we still have to go. Nonetheless, as Marx asserted over a century ago at the foundation of the International Workingmen's Association, "The emancipation of the working class must be the work of the working class itself."

## NOTES

[1]Quotations from Marcuse and Popper which are not footnoted are taken from the debate contained within this volume.

[2]On the basic assumptions of liberalism and the market society, cf., especially, C. B. Macpherson, *Democratic Theory: Essays in Retrieval* (Oxford, 1973), pp. 4-6.

[3]This rather unorthodox version of the concept of exploitation as the "net transfer of powers" from one class to the other was first used, to my knowledge, by Macpherson, *Democratic Theory*, p. 9.

[4]I have discussed in detail Marx's repudiation of philosophy in *The Betrayal of Marx* (New York, 1975), pp. 14-29.

[5]Agnes Heller, *Towards a Marxist Theory of Value* (Carbondale, Il., 1972), p. 19.

[6]Marcuse has explored the extent of these changes in *Eros and Civilization* (New York, 1962).

[7]For a discussion of man's "human" or "higher-level" needs, cf. Mihailo Marković, *From Affluence to Praxis* (Ann Arbor, 1973), pp. 91-92 *passim.*

[8]*Eros and Civilization*, pp. 180-202.

[9]Cf. Ernest Mandel, *Marxist Economic Theory* (New York, 1970), 2:605-89 for a stimulating treatment of these issues in a concrete, non-utopian manner.

[10] Georg Lukacs, *History and Class-Consciousness* (London, 1968), p. 292.

[11] Cf. *The Betrayal of Marx*, pp. 279-92, 298-314, 321-27, 354-78, 411-28.

[12] *History and Class-Consciousness*, p. 292.

[13] Cf. Marcuse, *One-Dimensional Man* (Boston, 1964), pp. 132-33.

[14] Cf. Karl Marx and Friederich Engels, *The German Ideology*, vol. 2 and *The Communist Manifesto*, part 3, for the classic Marxist polemic against utopianism.

[15] Walter Benjamin, *Illuminations* (New York, 1968), p. 260.

[16] Cf. Marx's schematic treatment of the transition from the "realm of necessity" to the "realm of freedom" in *Capital* (Moscow, 1966), 3:820.

[17] Marx, *Grundrisse* (New York, 1973), pp. 705-706, 708.

[18] *The Poverty of Historicism* (New York, 1961), p. 3.

[19] *Ibid.*, pp. vi-viii.

[20] *Ibid.*, p. 74.

[21] "Karl Popper and Historical Laws," in *Studies in Critical Philosophy* (Boston, 1973), pp. 197 ff.

[22] Part of the difficulty in getting to the bottom of Popper's critique of Marxism is that it is directed against the vulgar Marxism of the Second International, including the Austro-Marxists whom Popper had studied in his youth, and so-called "dialectical materialism," the philosophical ideology of the Soviet Union. Cf. *The Betrayal of Marx*, pp. 1-52 *passim*.

[23] *The Poverty of Historicism*, p. 67. The quotations are taken from Mannheim's *Ideology and Utopia* (New York, 1936), described here by Popper as "the most elaborate exposition of a holistic and historicist programme known to me."

[24] Plekhanov went furthest in tempering his determinism with a recognition of the element of contingency introduced by individual human agents, as is illustrated in his *The Role of the Individual in History* (New York, 1940). It is also important to recognize that, despite their theoretical determinism, both Lenin and Stalin were voluntarists in praxis. On this, cf. *The Betrayal of Marx*, pp. 44, 324-26.

[25] *The Eighteenth Brumaire of Louis Bonaparte* (Moscow, n.d.), p. 15.

[26] "Private Property and Communism," in *Karl Marx: The Essential Writings*, ed. F. Bender (New York, 1972), p. 89.

[27] *History and Class-Consciousness*, pp. 122-23.

[28] Maurice Merleau-Ponty, "The Metaphysical in Man," in *Sense and Non-Sense* (Evanston, Il., 1964), p. 92n.

[29] Merleau-Ponty, "Concerning Marxism," *ibid.*, p. 120.

[30] Our discussion of the significance of Galileo's work largely follows Husserl's argument in *The Crisis of the European Sciences and Transcendental Phenomenolgy* (Evanston, Il., 1970), pp. 21-59.

[31] That is, until an *objective* science of "subjectivity" (psychology) could be developed.

[32] Cf. Husserl, *Ibid.*, pp. 48-53, 111-14 *passim*; Martin Heidegger, *Being and Time* (New York, 1962), pp. 95-134; Enzo Paci, *The Function of the Sciences and the Meaning of Man* (Evanston, Il., 1972), pp. 19-24; Erwin Straus, *The Primary World of the Senses* (New York, 1963), pp. 158-86; and especially Merleau-Ponty, *The Phenomenology of Perception* (London, 1965), pp. 207-42 *passim*.

[33] "Concerning Marxism," in *Sense and Non-Sense*, p. 112.

[34] G. W. F. Hegel, *The Phenomenology of Mind* (London, 1961), p. 282. I have altered Baillie's translation somewhat.

[35] *History and Class-Consciousness*, p. 6.

[36] *Capital* (Moscow, 1965), 1:71-83.

[37] *Ibid.*, p. 185, italics added.

[38] *The Poverty of Historicism*, p. 74.

[39] "The Metaphysical in Man," in *Sense and Non-Sense*, p. 90.

[40] *The Open Society and Its Enemies* (New York, 1963), 2:41.

[41] Max Horkheimer, "The Authoritarian State (1940)," in *Telos* 15 (Spring, 1973), 11.

[42] Letter to Arnold Ruge, September, 1843, in *The Essential Writings*, p. 41.

[43] *History and Class-Consciousness*, p. 9. The citation from Marx is from *The Poverty of Philosophy* (Moscow, 1966), p. 96.

[44] Friedrich Engels, *Dialectics of Nature* (Moscow, 1966), p. 62.

[45] *History and Class-Consciousness*, p. 27.

[46] *Ibid.*, p. 7.

[47] *Ibid.*, p. 11.

[48] In this discussion of the "interest" of the sciences, I am dealing with the problem raised by J. Habermas in *Science and Human Interests* (Boston, 1971).

[49] *History and Class-Consciousness*, p. 14.

[50] *The Essential Writings*, p. 43.

[51] Popper, *The Poverty of Historicism*, pp. 91-92.

[52] Marx, third "Thesis on Feuerbach," in *The Essential Writings*, p. 153.

[53] But the struggle is still at a very rudimentary stage, characterized by widespread but not politicized discontent and utterly lacking in radical political tradition. The immediate and compelling need, therefore, is to develop a revolutionary consciousness; unless political discussion, criticism, and organization take place on a sustained, large scale, as was begun – but only begun – in the recent antiwar movement, socialist politics will be mere sectarianism. This points to the enormous task of the intellectuals and artists in raising the level of national political consciousness – a task which itself must begin with an attack on manipulative mass culture as a form of domination. They must show that the widespread discontent and protests, for example the outcry over the destruction of our environment, are implicitly socialist, and that until the social structure is radically changed only minor concessions can be gained. This is not to say that intellectual work can substitute for revolutionary work among the proletariat. By no means: it is rather to insist on an important precondition for that revolutionary work, without which it would be in vain.

[54] Needless to say, this point is controversial. Two classic statements on the necessity of violence are by L. Trotsky, *Terrorism and Communism* (Ann Arbor, 1969), and Frantz Fanon, *The Wretched of the Earth* (New York, 1965). In this context the classic positions against violence are to be found in Karl Kautsky, *The Dictatorship of the Proletariat* (Ann Arbor, 1964), and, from an ethical standpoint, Albert Camus, *The Rebel* (New York, 1956).

# THE THESES

*Herbert Marcuse:*

Late capitalist society is the wealthiest and most technically advanced in history. It offers—or should offer—the greatest and most tangible opportunities for a peaceful and liberated human existence. But at the same time it is a society that most effectively represses these opportunities for peace and liberation. This repression prevails today in society as a whole and consequently can be removed only by a radical transformation in the structure of this society.

*Sir Karl Popper:*

In all the social orders of which we know there have been injustice and repression, poverty and destitution; and our western democratic societies are no exceptions to this. But with us these evils are combatted. And I believe that there is less injustice and repression here, less poverty and destitution, than in any other social order we know of.

Our western democratic societies, then, are very imperfect and in need of reform, but they are the best ever. Further reforms are imperative. But of all political ideas the wish to make man perfect and happy is perhaps the most dangerous. The attempt to realize heaven on earth has invariably produced hell.

# POLITICAL AUTOBIOGRAPHY

## I

## HERBERT MARCUSE

I was born a Berliner and for some reason I'm still glad of that today—probably because of the Berliners' famous sense of humor or some such thing. However, my experience really began in 1918 with the German revolution. In 1918, I was briefly a member of the Soldiers Council in Berlin-Reinickendorf. I left this Soldiers Council when they began to elect former officers as a matter of course. Then I saw the revolution defeated in Berlin, partly through betrayal, partly through force. From Berlin I went to study at Freiburg and from 1928 to 1932—an interval broken only by a not very productive period in business in Berlin—I studied there under Husserl and Heidegger.

INTERVIEWER:  During that time you didn't join any communist organization. Why didn't you?

MARCUSE:  I didn't join any, and it you ask me why I must confess to my shame that I can give you no answer. I simply don't know. By 1919, when I went from Berlin to Freiburg, life in Freiburg was completely unpolitical. Then when I came back to Berlin the communist party was already split. I detected foreign influence—Russian influence—which I didn't consider exactly beneficial, and that may be one of the reasons why I didn't join. Nevertheless I became more and more politicized during this period. It was evident that fascism was coming, and that led me to an intensive study of Marx and Hegel. Freud came somewhat later. All this I did with the aim of understanding just why, at a time when the conditions for an authentic revolution were present, the revolution had collapsed or been defeated, the old forces had come back to power, and the whole business was beginning all over again in degenerate form. In 1933—it might even have been the end of December, 1932—I emigrated. I had been invited to teach at Horkheimer's *Institut fur Sozialforschung*. I went to Switzerland first for about a year, then in July, 1934, I moved to the United States. There I was employed at Columbia University where I also gave lectures. In 1940, I went to Washington so I could work during the war—that is, speaking plainly, to do everything that was in my power to help defeat the Nazi regime.

*INTERVIEWER:* Critics have reproached you for your cooperation at that time with the OSS, the American secret service. What exactly did you do there?

*MARCUSE:*  I was a political analyst. The division of the OSS that I was working in was a sort of research institute that was supposed to examine political developments in the countries involved in the war. I was responsible for central western Europe. If critics reproach me for that, it only shows the complete ignorance of these people, who seem to have forgotten that the war then was a war against fascism and that, consequently, I haven't the slightest reason for being ashamed of having assisted in it. I would like to add right away that I remained in Washington after the war as well. The main reason was that my wife fell ill with cancer and we couldn't leave.

During this time, that is, approximately from 1945 to 1949, I worked in bureaus in which my friends and I did everything we could to counteract policies that were becoming ever more blatantly anti-communist. There again my critics appear to have forgotten that McCarthy's attacks during this period were aimed directly against these groups within the State Department. Not because they were too nationalistic, but because in his opinion they were communist. Only after the war did I have a regular teaching post, first at Brandeis University, then at the University of California at San Diego. During recent years, let's say from about 1963-64, my philosophy—my general position—has become increasingly more radical because I thought I saw my past experience being repeated in this country too. Politics was veering to the extreme right, democracy was being eroded, the oppression of minorities was increasing, and an aggressive foreign policy was being pursued which had already led to two so-called "limited" wars. I thought I should do whatever I could as an intellectual to oppose this trend and that gave me some part in the student movement, a part which, although in my opinion, a very small one— I'll discuss this again later—is still assigned to me today on a much reduced scale. In 1969, I did not apply for a renewal of my position at the university because it was made clear to me beforehand that it would not be granted. All through 1969-70—in fact, also in 1968-69—I was receiving threatening letters almost regularly, even death threats. Just recently this has started up again in connection with the Angela Davis case, since she was, of course, my student. But I intend to stay here for the time being to write and do what I can.

## II

## SIR KARL POPPER

I became a Marxist around 1915, when I was thirteen years old, and an anti-Marxist in 1919, shortly before my seventeenth birthday. But I remained a socialist until I was thirty years old although I doubted more and more that freedom and socialism were compatible.

One experience was of decisive importance in making an anti-Marxist of me. It was in Vienna, the city where I was born. During a demonstration by young, unarmed socialist and communist workers, shots were fired and a few of the young workers were killed. I was horrified and disgusted with the police, but also with myself, for I felt that as a Marxist I was at least in principle partly to blame for the calamity, since Marxist theory demands the sharpening and intensification of the class struggle. It maintains that we will arrive at socialism all the more quickly the more the class struggle is intensified—that the revolution does indeed demand sacrifices but that capitalism demands more every day than the whole socialist revolution.

That is what Marxism says. But I asked myself whether we could actually know such a thing. I began to read Marx critically, and I discovered how little founded was the Marxist belief in an evil dominant social system, in so-called late capitalism and in the historically necessary advent of socialism.

What really existed were human beings and their joys and sorrows. I was an individualist in the sense that it was clear to me that it is between separate individuals that justice should exist, and that concepts such as those of "humanity," or even "class," are abstractions that can sometimes become very dangerous. For what are we to say of those Marxists who are ready to sacrifice concrete individuals for the sake of an abstract humanity? They believe that the worse off human beings become, the better it is for the revolution and consequently for humanity. To be sure, there are sharp conflicts of interest, but it is highly doubtful that the intensification of these conflicts leads to a better society, or to a worse one—for example, a fascist society.

At first, my critique of Marxism did not shake my socialist convictions in the slightest. For me, socialism was an ethical postulate—nothing more than the idea of justice. A social order in which there was great poverty and great wealth seemed to me unjust and intolerable. But as I realized more and more that state socialism makes the state too clumsy and gives bureaucrats too much power over the citizens, I gave up my socialist convictions. After that I no longer believed that socialism was compatible with freedom.

When I was twenty-eight I got a position in Vienna as a primary school teacher. In the meantime I had written much, but published scarcely anything. Spurred on by friends, I wrote two books. The second was published in 1934 under the title *Logik der Forschung*, or *The Logic of Scientific Discovery*. With this book I was launched into academic life. At that time a fascist dictatorship was in power in Austria; moreover, it was clear to me that Hitler would soon forcibly annex Austria. As I am of Jewish descent, I resolved to emigrate. My book brought me an invitation to lecture in England, and in 1936, on Christmas Eve, I was invited to teach in New Zealand. When I learned there, in March of 1938, of Hitler's march into Austria, I resolved to publish my critique of Fascism and Marxism, that is, my book *The Open Society and Its Enemies.*

In early 1945 I was invited to come from New Zealand to England, and from 1946 to 1969 I taught at London University. In between times I was visiting professor in America, and also for short periods in Austria, Japan, and Australia. For a year now I have been in retirement—or whatever they call it—but I'm working harder than ever.

# CRITIQUE AND PROGRAM

## I

## HERBERT MARCUSE: THE NEW SOCIETY

It has been asserted, and the statement has even been attributed to me, that highly developed late capitalist society, particularly in the United States, is no longer really a class society; that the gap between rich and poor has become smaller and the class struggle no longer takes place; that the system has succeeded in removing or in any case dampening the contradictions that Marx revealed. This is out of the question and I have never maintained it. The fact is that in the last few years the gap between rich and poor has become greater than ever before. The fact is that the contradictions, the inner contradictions of the capitalist system, continue to exist. They are manifested particularly sharply, far more sharply than before, in the general contradiction between the enormous wealth of society that could make a life without poverty and alienated labor really possible, and the repressive and destructive manner in which this social wealth is employed and distributed. Even the class struggle goes forward, although for the time being it does so in a purely economic form—wage demands, demands for the improvement of working conditions, demands which at the moment can still be met within the framework of the capitalist system, although their satisfaction is becoming more and more difficult within this given framework as we see from the great strikes of recent years and from inflation.

On the other hand, it is correct that late capitalist society displays important differences from earlier periods and that these differences lie essentially in what I have called the integration of the majority of the working class into the existing system; an integration which in its most pronounced form I should again limit to the society of the United States.

This integration of the working class sometimes goes so far that the working class can actually be characterized as a pillar of the establishment—particularly insofar as its union leadership and its support of American foreign policy are concerned. This integration is by no means merely superficial or ideological: there are very good reasons for it. Thanks in particular to the remarkable productivity of labor, late capitalism has succeeded in raising the standard of living for the majority of the population. Most workers, most skilled workers anyway, are very much better off today than they were before. Indeed, to a great extent they share the comforts of the so-called consumer society and it is quite understandable, quite rational, and definitely more than a result of propagandistic indoctrination or brainwashing, that they are not willing to give up these relative advantages for an alternative "Socialism" which in its pure state seems a utopia to them, or else looks like it does today in the Soviet Union and its satellite states.

So it is that, on the basis of this growing productivity of labor and the constantly increasing abundance of commodities, a manipulation and regulation of consciousness and the unconscious has commenced, which for late capitalism has become one of its most necessary control mechanisms. Again and again new needs have to be aroused to bring the people to buy the latest commodities and to convince them that they actually have a need for these commodities, and that these commodities will satisfy their need. The consequence is that people are completely delivered up to the fetishism of the world of commodities and in this way reproduce the capitalist system even in their needs. The commodities have to be bought because everyone else buys them and because in actual fact a need for these commodities has been stimulated and aroused.

This means that they have to be paid for, and as commodities are always getting more expensive, it also means that the struggle for existence is becoming ever more intensive, even though a rational distribution of labor and social wealth could reduce and lighten its burden to an extent never before possible. But exactly the reverse tendency is present in late capitalism. Precisely because of the accumulated social wealth, the struggle for existence is intensified and does not become any easier. The integration of the workers continues, but as I said, I think it is weakening. I believe the inner contradictions already are far more apparent today than they were a year ago and that even among the so-called middle classes—the bourgeoisie—the awareness is spreading that the relative prosperity that exists in the so-called consumer society is perhaps too dearly bought. Too dearly bought, not only because of the inhuman mind and body-killing work that a highly mechanized and more or less automated industry requires today, where a worker does nothing more for eight hours than turn the same screw or press the same button or attach the same part to another part. These mind and body-killing activities

are far too high a price when one considers that this
sort of struggle for existence is no longer really necessary today, and that thanks to the present social
wealth and the possiblity of rationally exploiting and
distributing available resources, most of this work
could be abolished; that is, it could be automated. Of
course this would involve the abolition of the greater
part of the insane waste that prevails in the so-called
consumer society in the interest of the most urgent
objective, namely, the abolition of the poverty and
misery which continue to exist and to be reproduced
unceasingly in highly developed capitalist society.

Another aspect that shows that the price of the
consumer society is exhorbitant is the increasingly
evident fact that stability and prosperity in the United
States are necessarily accompanied by new colonial
wars and the impoverishment and destruction of large
areas of the third world. This is a critique of the consumer society which shows that the Marxist analysis is
still valid today, but that a few fundamental concepts
of Marxist analysis, particularly the concept of the
proletariat, need to be differently formulated.

There is yet another, and, at least at first sight,
extraordinarily important defense of high capitalist
society; namely, that it maintains democracy and
despite everything preserves a large measure of pluralism. Now of course one has to admit, because it is a
fact, that there is still more freedom in the United
States of America today than, for example, in the
Soviet Union, and certainly infinitely much more than
in the new facist and semi-fascist dictatorships that are
springing up all over the world. On the other hand,
one cannot overlook the degree to which this democracy is a manipulated and limited democracy. There
is no real opposition in this country, in the sense that

such an opposition could make use of the mass media. There is, for example, not one real opposition newspaper such as those in France or Italy. The Left, the radical Left, has no adequate access to the mass media at all because it simply cannot raise the enormous amount of money necessary to purchase equal time on the television networks and the radio. From the very beginning, the Left is at a disadvantage in this democracy. In addition, it is a well-known fact that the political process is monopolized by the two big party machines here, the Democrats and the Republicans, that these two parties are fundamentally identical in all their objectives, and that therefore there can be no question here of a real democracy that is nourished from below.

This tendency for democracy to be parceled out between dominant parties which are fundamentally united in their objectives and policies is of course most advanced in the United States, but I believe a similar tendency can also be seen very clearly in Europe, especially in England and probably also in the Federal Republic of Germany.

*INTERVIEWER:*  What then does the alternative model of society look like?

*MARCUSE:*  Well, the question of an alternative always seemed a very simple one to me, and it still does today. What young people want today is a society without war, without exploitation, without repression and poverty and waste. Now, advanced industrial society has at its disposal all the technical, scientific, and natural resources that are necessary to construct such a society in reality. And all that is preventing this liberation is the existing system and the interests that work day and night defending this system, employing increasingly violent means to do so. The alternative model does not seem to me so very difficult to define. How it should be concretized is another question again. But I believe that as a result of the abolition of poverty, massive waste, and destruction of resources, a way of life can be found in which human beings can truly determine their own existence.

*INTERVIEWER:*   And what is the road to this society like?

*MARCUSE:*   The road to this society—that, of course, is something that can become concrete only in the course of the struggle for this society. The first thing to say about it is that it will be a different road in different countries according to their various stages of development: development of the productive forces, of consciousness, political tradition, etc. I should like to limit my comments to the United States because I know this country best. I emphasize from the outset that the situation in France and Italy, for example, is very different. There is, of course, the question of the agent of change, the question "Who is the revolutionary subject?" This question seems unreasonable to me because the revolutionary subject can only evolve in the process of change itself. It is not a thing that is simply there and that one has only to find somehow. The revolutionary subject originates in praxis, in the development of consciousness, the development of action.

INTERVIEWER: Could this agent today be the working class?

MARCUSE: I have been reproached for saying the working class is no longer a revolutionary subject. That is, of course, a falsification of what I said. What I said is that the working class in the United States today is not a revolutionary subject. That is no value judgment on my part; it is, I believe, simply a statement of fact, a description. And again the situation is very different in France and Italy, where strong political traditions exist among the working class, where the standard of living has not yet reached the high level of the United States, and where consequently the radical potential of the working class is much greater than in the United States.

INTERVIEWER: You have always very strongly emphasized the role of the students. What role do they play in a changing society?

MARCUSE: I have never maintained that the student movement today has replaced the workers' movement as a possible re-

volutionary subject. What I have said is
that the student movement functions
today as a catalyst, as a forerunner of
the revolutionary movement and that
today this is an extraordinarily crucial
role. I believe that all these defeatist
remarks to the effect that a movement
of intellectuals which is limited mostly
to universities and colleges cannot be a
revolutionary movement, and that it is
only a movement of intellectuals, a so-
called elite—these remarks simply by—I
pass the facts. That is, in the universities and colleges of today, the cadre
of a future society is being educated
and trained, and because of this the
development of consciousness, of critical thinking in the universities and
colleges, is a crucial task.

INTERVIEWER:   What can revolution start from today?
Presumably no longer poverty, at least
not in the advanced countries.

MARCUSE:   That depends completely on the various
countries. In countries where poverty
prevails, it will naturally play a crucial
role. In other countries, it will not. Probably the crucial characteristic of revolution in the twentieth or twenty-
first century is that it is born not pri-
marily out of privation, but—let us
say—out of the general inhumanity, dehumanization, and disgust at the waste
and excess of the so-called consumer
society; that is, out of disgust at the

brutality and ignorance of human beings. Because of this, the chief demand of this revolution will be—really for the first time in history—to find an existence worthy of human beings and to construct a completely new form of life. This is a question then, not only of quantitative change, but also of real qualitative change.

*INTERVIEWER:* Revolution out of disgust—isn't that really an un-Marxist thought?

*MARCUSE:* It's not an un-Marxist thought at all, for there are very strong objective and social reasons for disgust. Disgust is indeed only the expression of a contradiction, of the ever growing contradiction that permeates capitalist society, namely, the contradiction between the enormous wealth of society and its wretched and destructive employment. At a high level of consciousness this contradiction expresses itself as disgust with the existing society.

*INTERVIEWER:* Professor, is a humane, emancipated society actually unattainable through reforms?

*MARCUSE:* Reforms can and must be attempted. Everything that can serve to alleviate poverty, misery, and repression must be attempted. But exploitation and repression belong to the essence of capitalist production just as war and the concentration of economic power do. That means sooner or later the point is reached where reforms run up against the limits of the system; where to put through reforms would be to sever the roots of capitalist production—namely profit.

That is the point at which the system will defend itself, must defend itself, against reforms in the interests of self-preservation, and where the question then arises: "Is revolution possible?"

INTERVIEWER: Roughly, how will the emancipated, post-revolutionary society be organized? Can the complex society of the western industrial countries, for example, be constructed along the lines of a council system while preserving its efficiency and technological standards?

MARCUSE: We cannot prescribe today what the organizational forms of post-revolutionary society will actually look like. It would be senseless to do that. We are not free, and as such, we cannot predetermine how free human beings would arrange their life and society. We can, of course, adumbrate a few of the fundamental institutions. The "council system" is of course, historically a very loaded term. But I believe the basic idea is still valid. I said that in a free society human beings determine their life, their existence. The first thing that is part of this is that they determine how the socially necessary labor is to be divided and for what objectives it is to be performed. At first this would probably best be done in local and regional assemblies, committees, councils, or whatever you want to call them; being on the spot, they would know best what priorities are to be fixed and how the necessary social labor is to be allocated.

INTERVIEWER: But who can guarantee that the abolition of the capitalist mode of production will lead to a society in which the individual is free and can realize himself? At all events the existing socialist societies don't justify this confidence.

MARCUSE: There is no guarantee for it. History is not a insurance agency. One can't expect guarantees. What one can say on the subject is that the abolition of capitalist society in any case can and will provide the foundation upon which a free society could grow.

INTERVIEWER: What concrete political actions should the New Left take today? Would you recommend a policy of alliance between this group and other critical but non-Marxist forces? For example, with parliamentary forces?

MARCUSE: The question must be answered differently according to the degree of development in the various capitalist countries. Where the counterrevolution is already at work, a policy of alliance is necessary. But for the New Left this can only be temporary and cannot become a political principle! And it can only be directed at specific targets in specific situations, for instance, demonstrations and local elections. And beyond that? I think that today all radical opposition is extra-parliamentary opposition.

INTERVIEWER: May the New Left employ violence as well in its extra-parliamentary actions against the ruling system?

MARCUSE: Well, I do not think this question can be discussed in a general conversation such as this but only within the circle of participants and with an eye toward definite situations. In general, on the question of violence I can only repeat what I have already said; that in existing society violence is institutionalized to an absolutely monstrous extent and the primary question is first of all, "From whom does the violence come?" In any event, I believe we can say that—at least in a period of incipient counterrevolution—violence comes first of all from the existing society and that from this point of view the opposition is confronted with the question of counterviolence, the violence of defense but definitely not the violence of aggression.

*INTERVIEWER:* One last question. Are you not pre-supposing in your emancipated society a new anthropological structure of man? A human being who always does good, a human being who always acts in solidarity?

*MARCUSE:* No, I don't think so. What I am presuming is not a human being who always does good and always acts in solidarity, but a human being who first of all, and perhaps for the first time in history, really can act in solidarity and do good. I believe that on the basis of the achievements of industrial society the possibility is provided to emancipate extensively the instincts repressed in the interests of domination, and that through these emancipated instincts—essentially the life instincts and not the destructive instincts—something like solidarity can, in fact, become reality for the first time in history. For the life instincts are opposed to the aggressive instincts: they contain, in fact, the germ of the possibilites and conditions necessary for an improvement of life, for a greater enjoyment of life, and indeed, not against others, but with them.

## II

## SIR KARL POPPER: THE OPEN SOCIETY

During 1935 and 1936 I visited England for the first time. I came from Austria where a relatively mild dictatorship was in power, but was threatened by its National Socialist neighbor. In the free air of England I could breathe again. It was as if the windows had been opened. The name "Open Society" comes from this experience.

What do I see as characteristic of an open society? I would like to make two points. First, that in an open society there is the possibility of free discussion and that discussion has influence on politics. Second, that institutions exist for the protection of freedom and the weak. Let us take the second point first.

The state protects its citizens from brute force through legal and social institutions and it can also protect them from abuse by economic power. That protection is already in effect and it can be improved. We must construct social institutions that will protect the economically weak from the strong, that is, institutions that can counter exploitation. For political power can control economic power. The Marxists underestimate the possibilities of politics and in particular what they call "formal freedom."

I would therefore stress the central role of political institutions for social reform. What is important is not so much *who* governs as *how* the rulers are influenced and controlled.

With this I return to my first point, the significance of public discussion. Of those countries with a more of less open social order, the United States is the most important; on its fate all the others depend. Barely a hundred years have passed since the freeing of the slaves in America—since the bloody civil war between North and South that lasted almost five years. This was a terrible crisis for the country, a crisis of conscience. Today the United States is in a similar crisis of conscience over the Negro problem once again and at the same time over Vietnam.

Here we see clearly what is most important for the openness of a society; freedom of opinion, the existence of an opposition. The biggest newspapers, along with the most influential radio and television commentators, are strongly in opposition. The opposition demands the withdrawal of the American armed forces from Vietnam and under its influence the government has accepted this as a program. Here we have a unique event that is conceivable only in an open society. After a war that has lasted for years, public discussion forces the government to admit that the war was a grave error and that it must be terminated as soon as possible.

Of course I don't want to set up American democracy as an ideal. America is a country in which there is far too much violence and crime. Since the murder of President Kennedy, America has changed remarkably quickly. Previously the atmosphere was hopeful but now the country is in a depression deepened even more by the murders of Martin Luther King and Robert Kennedy and by the war in Vietnam. Americans are no longer sure that their country and form of government are the best. These violent deeds are perhaps in part a consequence of the American tradition, but they are not a consequence of the form of government or of the so-called system of domination. In fact, forms of life and beliefs change very rapidly in America: open societies are not very stable precisely because they are exposed to critical discussion. Dictatorships are more stable, and, naturally, even more so are utopias, which are always depicted as being static.

INTERVIEWER: You say the state can protect its citizens from economic power by means of political institutions. It certainly could do so, but Marxists maintain to the contrary that precisely these institutions are occupied by the ruling groups and are therefore ineffective.

POPPER: I consider that to be immeasurably exaggerated. Naturally in a democracy every institution is sometimes occupied by one group and sometimes by another. That's plain enough. But the idea that the institutions in a democracy are, so to speak, continually occupied by the bourgeoisie is nothing more than a form of the Marxist fairy tale of the class dictatorship: that every state is a dictatorial state and that so-called formal democracy is nothing more than a class dictatorship. As I say, I consider that a fairy tale.

INTERVIEWER: But are not at least *elements* of a *class society* evident when, for example, in the Federal Republic of Germany 70% of new private wealth goes to the smallest occupational group, the financially independent, while the group that is seven times larger, the employees, have to make do with the remaining 30%? When the tax system one-sidedly favors a small class? When the owners of capital, without any effort of their own, keep on accumulating wealth while the bulk of employees have to consume their income entirely and so can never become owners of capital at all?

POPPER:    You are posing several questions here at once. The word "class" can have many misleading meanings. The Marxists maintain that all democracies are disguised class dictatorships, but this misleading claim has little to do with the existence of great differences in wealth. For we can conceive of a free society with equal opportunities for all—where everyone has the same education, and inheritance taxes distribute all fortunes equally—in which, nevertheless, there prove to be great differences in newly produced wealth. As long as there is no poverty, that is scarcely to be regarded as an evil: large fortunes are, of course, nearly always invested and they make it possible to try out innovations. There might be, however, not only rich people but poor people as well in this society; that would then be a great evil. But nevertheless the rich and the poor would not be classes in the Marxist sense.

But your remark referred to the Federal Republic of Germany and you complain that in it new fortunes are very unevenly distributed. That proves little about its class character and nothing about a class dictatorship. You assert also that the tax system one-sidedly favors a small class. If that is the case then there are *remedies* in a democracy, as can be seen from the English, and even the American, tax system. In Great Britian far more than half the national income goes to the state in the form of taxes: income tax, corporation tax, and indirect taxes. But it is probably because the tax burden is so heavy that the whole economy, including the worst-paid, suffer under it.

This demonstrates the untenability of the Marxist doctrine that all democracies are dictatorships in disguise. And although one can perhaps speak—as you do—of "elements of a class society," one can, on the other hand, also say that the various democracies realize varying degrees of approach to a classless society.

*INTERVIEWER:* Do you not think that the formal-democratic political structure can only be filled with life when it finds correspondences in the economic domain?

*POPPER:* Can the formal-democractic political structure be filled with life only when it finds correspondences in the eco-

nomic field? Perhaps I may trans-
late your question into a simpler
language—isn't the co-existence of
poverty and wealth an intolerable social
evil? My answer is that poverty is a
great evil and it becomes a greater evil
when it exists alongside great wealth.
But an even worse evil than the opposition of wealth and poverty is the
opposition between freedom and
slavery—the opposition between a New
Class, the ruling dictatorship, and its
undesirable fellow citizens, banished to
concentration camps or elsewhere.

So I see the greatest value of a
democracy in its opportunity for free
rational discussion and in the influence
of this critical discussion on politics. In
this I am strongly opposed to those
who believe in violence, particularly
Fascists. In a very similar manner revolutionary or neo-Marxists claim that
there is no "objective" discussion. They
say that before one enters into a discussion with someone, one must be
sure that he has the revolutionary
Marxist view of society, that is, that he
radically rejects the present so-called
"capitalist" society. That means a discussion of the major problems is impossible.

Fascist anti-intellectuals and revolutionary Marxists are therefore agreed
that one cannot and should not discuss
with an opponent. Both reject a critical
discussion of their positions.

But let us consider what this rejection means. It means the suppression of all opposition when one comes to power. It means the rejection of the open society, the rejection of freedom, and the adoption of a philosophy of violence.

Under the influence of these ideas both Marxists and neo-Marxists are blind to the achievements of democracy, which alone makes it possible for them to propagate their ideas. Their theory teaches them that political freedom is valueless or nearly valueless since, of course, it is nothing more than a dictatorship in disguise.

But this is quite unrealistic as can be seen from the fact that the most recent revival of Marxism has taken place in all the open societies of the West—and in these only. Democracies are always open to ideas and, in particular, to opposing ideas. Far from being dictatorships in disguise, these democracies are always ready to doubt themselves. They know very well that much is not as it should be. Ideas have an opportunity to triumph only in open societies, and the Marxists who believe that democracies are only dictatorships in disguise don't see that all dictatorships, whether of the Right or the Left, are essentially the same.

This is a consequence of false theories that make them blind to the significance of the critical struggle of ideas—of critical discussion.

*INTERVIEWER:* Professor, your "Open Society" presupposes a pluralism of power, an equal opportunity for all, that indeed exists in the constitutions of the Western democracies but not unconditionally in their political reality. Do you believe the "open society" exists already, or must it first be built?

*POPPER:* I believe it is both reality and ideal. There are, of course, various degrees of openness. In one democracy the society will be more mature, more advanced, and more open than in another democracy. How good or bad it is depends on several things: on its previous history, its tradition, its political institutions, its educational methods, and ultimately on the people, who alone give these institutions life. I would suggest that a rather sharp division be drawn between democracies and dictatorships. One lives in a democracy if there are institutions which make it possible to get rid of the government without the use of violence, that is, without shooting them. That is the characteristic of a democracy. But if one has a democracy there is still a long way to a really open society. That is a gradual process.

I believe in reason in the sense that I believe that we should all endeavor to assume an attitude such as I have described. Naturally I don't believe that this is easy to do or that all men are always rational; they are so only rarely. I also don't believe in the "Force of Reason" or the "Power of Reason." I believe, rather, that we have the choice between reason and violence; and I believe that reason is the only alternative to violence and that the avoidable use of violence is criminal.

But Marxists don't believe in reason, because they think that behind all arguments there are hidden only the selfish interests of men.

Now it is of course correct that the interests, in particular the economic interests, of men play a large part in politics. But it is surely quite plain that other things, too, play a part, for example, the desire to be just.

Marxist praxis is based on a highly sophisticated speculative theory and is to that extent not quite as anti-intellectual as fascist praxis. But really, it comes to the same thing: it is in practice anti-intellectual and irrational although it rests on a rather oversubtle theory.

Violence always leads to more violence. And violent revolutions kill the revolutionaries and destroy their ideals. The only survivors are those who are the most skillful adepts at surviving.

What a revolution from the Left would with certainty produce is the loss of freedom to criticize, to furnish opposition. Whether the resulting dictatorship is of the Left or Right depends partly on chance and is chiefly a difference in nomenclature. I maintain that only in a democracy, in an open society, do we have the possibility to redress grievances. If we destroy this social order through a violent revolution we will not only be responsible for the heavy sacrifices of the revolution but will create a state of affairs that will make the abolition of social evils, injustice, and repression impossible. I am for individual freedom and I hate the coercion of the state and the arrogance of government officials as much as anyone. But unfortunately the state is a necessary evil; without a state things won't work. And unfortunately the saying is true: the more people, the more state. Through violence mankind can easily be exterminated. What is necessary is to work for a more reasonable society in which conflicts are settled rationally, more and more. I say "more reasonable"! Strictly speaking, there is no reasonable society, but there is always one that is more reasonable than the existing one and toward which we should therefore strive. That is a realistic demand and no utopia!

# THEORETICAL BACKGROUND

## I

## HERBERT MARCUSE

*INTERVIEWER:*  Professor, behind your political program there of course stands a definite view of the nature of science. Let us discuss it briefly. First of all, are ethical-social norms in general justifiable purely scientifically, or are they based on subjective value judgments, which, while they may be carefully thought out, are ultimately not fully justifiable on rational grounds.

*MARCUSE:*  They are definitely not based on subjective value judgments. Everything depends here on what you mean by "science" and "scientific method." If you believe that the model of the natural sciences is the sole model of the method of science, then, certainly, the social sciences and the norms or values that are predominant in them are unscientific. But I consider the identification of scientific method with the model of the natural sciences to be either one-sided arrogance or simply false. There is a scientific method that rests on a critical analysis of the facts and embraces those realms that are not at all accessible to the methods of natural science and its quantification. I would even say that scientific method as it prevails in the social sciences, or, at least, should prevail, is in a certain sense even more exact and correct than the model of the natural sciences.

INTERVIEWER: So there are scientific procedures beyond empirical examinations and deductive logic?

MARCUSE: Beyond empirical examination and deductive logic—these embrace everything that could ever be imagined. Once again, I would say that the scientific method of the social sciences rests on a critical analysis of tendencies, historical possibilities that are in some way demonstrable. And that is the framework within which the social scientific method proceeds.

INTERVIEWER: May I infer from your answer that in contrast to traditional Marxists you do not assert the validity of something like the "dialectic" which is supposed to be a second kind of logic superior to deductive logic?

MARCUSE: Right! I see no sense in classifying the dialectic as a "subject" of the academic division of labor.

*INTERVIEWER:* What is the connection between theory and practice? Does it mean only that the scientist—the theorist—should also adopt a position on political questions, or more?

*MARCUSE:* You have just formulated the issue as a personal, private relation of theory to praxis. I believe there is an objective, essential relation between theory and praxis. For example, I believe the concepts of freedom, justice, humanity, and mankind, if actually analyzed and developed, include the struggle against existing slavery and exploitation against existing inhumanity. The connection between theory and practice is, therefore, an essential and internal one. Or expressed differently, theoretical concepts are false if they are not related to the sphere of praxis.

*INTERVIEWER:* Another point. The "bourgeois" understanding of democracy, the option for representative democracy, works from the assumption that there is no objective truth in politics—or only rarely—and that the system must therefore be kept open for new ideas. Marxism, which not only considers facts but also norms—political and moral valuation—to be demonstrable, might perhaps prevent the penetration of new ideas. Is there not latent here a dogmatic, not to say totalitarian, formula?

MARCUSE: It may be that representative democracy starts from the assumption that the system has to be kept open for new ideas. But what is it like in reality? If this assumption is meant seriously, it is not enough to give freedom of thought, freedom of speech, and freedom of the press. Objective and subjective conditions for the understanding and dissemination of ideas must also be granted or created. In the USA you can say and print practically anything you want. But, first, punishment won't be long in coming—loss of job, no promotion, surveillance, if necessary the police and the law court. Secondly, the pressure of the monopolized mass-media and general integration are so effective that freedom of speech and propaganda can still be tolerated—which speaks for the closure of the system, not for its openness. And yet we must, of course, welcome and defend this freedom of speech and of the press. It remains a necessary condition for our struggle and aims.

Now, as far as a truly socialist society is concerned, it will be open to new ideas—otherwise it is not socialist.

INTERVIEWER: Professor, do you share the view that Marxism is a closed system of thought in which all knowledge and postulates are rigorously derivable from the basic insights of dialectical and historical materialism? Or can Marxism also be understood as a sum of politico-moral postulates which might well be scientifically provable but which can nevertheless be detached from their traditional philosophic basis?

*MARCUSE:* Marxism is not a "closed system of thought." Its objectivity or general validity is that of history in which it is itself an active force and in which it develops—without surrendering its conceptual basis. This basis is the dialectical analysis of the social process from which results the human—not the natural!—necessity to change the society.

## II
## SIR KARL POPPER

INTERVIEWER: In *The Logic of Scientific Discovery* and *Conjectures and Refutations* you developed your theory of science, of "Critical Rationalism." Could you once again sketch its basic ideas here?

POPPER: Socrates says at one point in his famous apology, "I know that I know nothing and scarcely even that. Nevertheless the Delphic oracle has called me the wisest of men." And after some reflection Socrates finds the following solution: "I am conscious of my ignorance. Perhaps it is the consciousness of my narrow limits that makes me a little wiser than other mem who do not even know that they know nothing."

Socrates also said a politician or statesman ought to be wise. By this he meant: "A politician ought to be even more conscious of his ignorance than other men, for he has a grave responsibility. This responsibility ought to lead him to a realization of his own limitations and so to intellectual humility."

I agree with Socrates. And from this I can best formulate my basic objection to all modern Marxists. Marxists believe that they know a great deal. They are completely lacking in intellectual humility. They preen themselves with their knowledge and elaborate terminology.

This objection doesn't hold for Marx or Engels. They were great, original thinkers who had new ideas that were often difficult to formulate. It is up to anyone who has anything new and important to say to be understood. He will place the greatest value on writing as simply and intelligibly as he can. Nothing is easier than to write turbidly. But I accuse modern revolutionary Marxists of boasting and trying to impress us with few ideas and many words. Nothing is more alien to them than intellectual humility. They are not pupils of Socrates or even Kant, but of Hegel. Therefore I believe, like Socrates, that we know nothing or very little. Our ignorance is boundless. But that is evidently not everything. Naturally we cannot ignore the existence of the natural sciences and their splendid successes. But as we look at these sciences rather more closely, we find that they do not consist of positive or certain knowledge, but of bold hypotheses that we continuously improve through sharp criticism or else eliminate entirely. This amounts to a step by step approach to truth. But we have no positive, certain knowledge. There is but hypothetical knowledge.

And above all, there is scientific progress. For critical discussion of our hypotheses always assesses these hypotheses from the position that we prefer those that seem to us a better approximation to the truth and that stand up better to our attempts at refutation.

Therefore in science there is no point of equilibrium, no point at which we can say, "Now we have reached the truth," but only bold hypothetical theories that we attempt to criticize and replace with better ones.

In science, therefore, we have the rule: the more scientific revolutions, the better. For the history of science, therefore, the Marxian battle cry "Permanent revolution!" actually holds good.

Because of this, people have charged me with inconsistency, saying that a revolutionary theory of science of this sort ought logically to make me a political revolutionary. But this is a serious misunderstanding. It is exactly this radicalism in the intellectual domain, the bold invention of new revolutionary theories and the revolutionary overthrow of old theories, that enables us to avoid violence in the field of praxis. To make this proposition more comprehensible I would like to compare the struggle for existence in the animal and plant world with the "struggle for existence" of our hypotheses.

Plants and animals produce changes or mutations, and the mutations that make possible adaptation to the conditions of life are picked out by natural selection. But that means no more than that the less well adapted or poor mutations are thereby eliminated; that those plants and animals that are bearers of these poor mutations are wiped out—either they don't survive or else they produce so few offspring that they finally die out. An hypothesis can be compared to a mutation. Instead of producing new mutations men sometimes produce new hypotheses or theories. If men are uncritical, the supporters of unadapted or poor hypotheses are wiped out.

But rational, critical discussion enables us to criticize our hypotheses and eliminate false ones without destroying the inventors or representatives of poor hypotheses. That is the great achievement of the critical method. It makes it possible to recognize hypotheses as erroneous and to condemn them without condemning their supporters.

The method of critical discussion lets our hypotheses die for us, while the uncritical method of fanatics consists in our engaging ourselves as martyrs for our hypotheses. Penetrating criticism, the critical examination of our hypotheses, replaces the violent struggle for existence. In the same way the revolutionary progress of our ideas, theories, or hypotheses can replace the violent revolutions that have demanded so much human sacrifice.

It is interesting that recently in Germany people who evidently don't quite understand what they are talking about have labeled me a positivist. Positivists are philosophers who are opposed to speculative theories: they want to stick as closely as possible to what is given and perceivable. Now, I always was an opponent of all dogmatism, and from my first publications on I have fought against this positivism. While positivism teaches: "Stay with what can be perceived," I teach: "Be bold in erecting speculative hypotheses but then criticize and examine them mercilessly."

*INTERVIEWER:*  So, Professor, you are demanding revolution in science and in thought, but not in political praxis. And you say science itself can never supply certain knowledge, but only hypotheses that for the time being have not been refuted. How does that look in the social field?

*POPPER:*  Exactly the same! In the social field too we have ideas and theories. We work out theories for the abolition of social evils, attempt to think out their consequences, and then judge the theories accordingly.

*INTERVIEWER:*  But what are these "social evils"? What

they are can only be measured against definite social values. How can it be proved which of these social postulates are correct and which are not?

POPPER: That can't be proved, just as nothing can be proved in the natural sciences. But it can be discussed. And one can compare various social attitudes with their consequences. In the last, final analysis, the acceptance or rejection of such a social value is a question of decision.

INTERVIEWER: So social axioms, the axioms of politics, can't ultimately be proved; one can only decide personally for or against them! In actual fact your whole idea of the "Open Society" is based on such a fundamental decision, namely, the decision in favor of rationality in the social field, too. Can you explain this in more detail?

POPPER: Rationalism prizes argument, theory, and the examination of experience. But one cannot justify this decision in favor of rationalism through argument and experience yet again. Although it can be discussed, it rests ultimately on an irrational decision, on the belief in reason. This decision in favor of reason, however, is not a purely intellectual one but a moral one as well. It influences our whole attitude toward other people and toward the problems of social life. Closely connected to it is the belief in the rational unity of man, in the value of every human being. Rationalism can be better united with a humanitarian attitude than can irrationalism with its rejection of equal rights. Admittedly, individual human beings are unequal in many respects, but that doesn't stand in the way of the claim for equality of treatment, for equal rights. "Equality before the law" is not a fact but a political demand which is based on a moral decision.

The belief in reason, as well as in the reason of other men, implies the idea of impartiality and tolerance, the idea of the rejection of every claim to authority.

# CONCLUSION

## I

## HERBERT MARCUSE

INTERVIEWER: What ultimate moral impulse animates the philosopher Herbert Marcuse, in committing himself so much to radical politics?

MARCUSE: Commit? Look, for me this is not some special commitment. It comes quite naturally, quite spontaneously. I simply cannot think today without, as a matter of course, thinking about what is going on around me, about what is happening in the world. And, indeed, not only in my immediate surroundings, but in the ghettos of the United States, in Southeast Asia, Latin America, everywhere that misery, cruelty, and repression stare one in the face. Even if one doesn't want to look one feels it, reads of it, knows it. I wouldn't say it is a special commitment for me; it is the natural expression of my existence.

## II
## SIR KARL POPPER

*INTERVIEWER:*    To conclude with the fundamental question yet again, Professor. Is revolution, the forcible instating of what is recognized as being better, unthinkable for you?

*POPPER:*    There one has to distinguish between a revolution against a democracy, including what Marxists term merely formal democracy, and a revolution against a real dictatorship, which unfortunately only rarely is able to get rid of the dictatorship. Also, the word "revolution" can refer both to a peaceful and to a violent overthrow. Marxism has left this ambiguity unresolved. And the unintended consequence of violent revolution is often dictatorship. So it was in the English revolution of the sevententh century which led to the dictatorship of Cromwell; in the French Revolution which led to Robespierre and Napoleon; and in the Russian Revolution which led to Stalin. It seems then that revolutionary ideals and their supporters almost always fall victim to the revolution. Nonviolent changes are something completely different. They enable us to take notice of the unwanted and undesirable consequences of our actions and to alter them in time, when such consequences are setting in. Through this they create both an atmosphere in which public criticism of existing social conditions cannot be suppressed by force, and a framework which makes further reforms possible.

# AFTERWORD TO THE GERMAN EDITION

by

Franz Stark

I

Herbert Marcuse and Karl Popper, the "grand old men" of the two great currents of philosophy in our time that aim at changing society, have met only briefly. They have never really had a serious discussion together, and it doesn't look as though they ever will. Nevertheless, confrontation between them is imperative. Only a social theory that deals critically with the contradictions between a revolutionary socialism and a movement for evolutionary social reform, and to some extent overcomes these contradictions, can be a truly critical theory.

Through the medium of television Bavarian Broadcasting has attempted to stage the confrontation between Marcuse and Popper that did not take place. The editor of these texts [in the German edition] has interviewed both political philosophers in their present homes and has fitted their answers together in contrapuntal fashion.

It was not easy to get Herbert Marcuse's final agreement to take part. Only a preliminary conversation during a visit to Germany and half a dozen letters from Munich to La Jolla, the garden suburb

of San Diego, California, where Marcuse lives, could
move the 72 year-old philosopher to a documentary
self-portrayal of his life and political philosophy.
When, in November 1969, the television crew was at
last able to track Marcuse down in his simple
wooden house close to the campus of his last university and high above the rocky coast of the Pacific
Ocean, he proved to be most cooperative—and a
master in the use of the medium.

Karl Raimund Popper—like his neo-Marxist opponent, retired since 1969—immediately accepted the
project. The scholar lives with his wife in seclusion
in Penn, in the English county of Buckinghamshire.
Four years younger than Marcuse, but in contrast to
him not of robust health, Popper must have experienced the medium and its demands as something
of a burden.

While Marcuse received world-wide publicity in the
mid-sixties as a theorist of the international protest
movement of the New Left, Karl Popper has been
little known outside the academic field. And this, although Sir Karl Popper—he was knighted in 1965—is
perhaps the most influential philosopher in Anglo-
Saxon and Scandinavian spheres of culture. In West
Germany, students began to pay attention to Popper
only after his confrontation in 1961 with Theodor
Adorno in Tubingen, with which he rekindled the so-
called "Positivismusstreit" in German sociology. That
since then the dialecticians of the "Frankfurt
School" label him a positivist is absurd, for as a
philosopher of science, Popper himself has formulated the most acute and penetrating critique of
the neo-positivism of Rudolf Carnap and the Vienna
Circle.

## II

More freedom, more justice, more humanity for the western democratic society and ultimately, of course, for the all societies of the world—this is the theme of both philosophers. When one carefully considers their contrasting plans for the future, one encounters first of all the *diagnosis* of present day society, the analytical core. Herbert Marcuse, who unlike traditional Marxists no longer deals exclusively with the political economy and class situation of society, but with the consciousness and instinctual structure of "One Dimensional Man," draws us a terrifying picture. But is our society in fact as repressive as the neo-Marxist claims? That the overwhelming majority of individuals does not experience the situation in this way would not be an objection for Marcuse. He would say that the headlong progress of technology, productivity, and the living standards of even the underprivileged inwardly and outwardly mask the barbaric by-products of late capitalism and deaden the consciousness of these individuals to such an extent that they can no longer comprehend their objective situation at all. As much sympathy as one may manifest for this theory, the question remains: how does Marcuse come to possess the criteria that distinguish "true" consciousness from "false" consciousness?

Nevertheless, if Marcuse's devastating critique were justified only in part, it would arouse mistrust of the relatively optimistic picture that Popper paints of this society. Admittedly, Popper recognizes throughout the injustice and inequalities that prevail. But he believes that, through state and social institutions, representative parliamentary democracy is ultimately in a position to defend its weak members against the strong ones.

The second stage in the plans of both philosophers is the *aim* of the society that they are striving for and the road to it. For Marcuse there is no doubt that his "New Society" will be socialist and that the road to it leads through the revolutionary overthrow of the late capitalist system. But differing once more from traditional Marxists, Marcuse demands first of all a radical transformation in consciousness, that is, in the "superstructure," before a revolutionary change occurs in the economic "base." This is socialism on a biological foundation: it is, one might say, Karl Marx enriched with Sigmund Freud.

What Marcuse wishes to attain here is nothing less than the creation of a new man who is pleasure oriented, who does not know the murderous competitive spirit of capitalism, who has lost his aggression and instead acts in solidarity; a man who hates war deeply; a utopia of seductive style to which one would yield all too willingly.

But many questions remain open. How is an industrialized society to be organized? Would not the required permanent revolution in human consciousness result in the politicization of all social intercourse with the individual losing almost all his freedom? Furthermore, can one be quite sure that Marcuse's revolution will not produce a dictatorship that he himself does not desire? The neo-Marxist replies: "There is no guarantee. History is not an insurance agency."

And as with his diagnosis of present day society, there arises with his plan for the "New Society" the question of what criteria justify the "correctness" of this society and how these criteria are arrived at. In the last analysis does there not lie hidden here a dogmatically elitist formula of "the idea of privileged access to the truth for those with the knowledge of salvation" (Hans Albert)?

Karl Raimund Popper, on the other hand, does not direct his gaze as far as utopia. His aim, the "Open Society," is the continuation of the progress of existing parliamentary democracy through social reform. For the neoliberal, every revolution carries the danger of "killing the revolutionaries and of destroying their ideals." Reforms, on the other hand, can be corrected if undesired consequences arise. The decisive question here, of course, is whether the "Open Society" can ever be realized if Marcuse's diagnosis of late capitalism is even close to being ture. Moreover, Popper demands a rational adjudication of social conflicts; but aren't values and political attitudes at least influenced by prevailing social conventions?

It is also noteworthy that Popper's "Open Society" is not really described in any substantial way. The liberal democrat Popper has no image of a "correct" society. He only gives the rules that are to be abided by in social conflicts and the institutional safeguards that must function. What political objectives are finally to be aimed at in compliance with those rules is something that must be continually worked out and (provisonally) established through critical discussion.

But how can this consensus be found in a society of conflicting interests? Practically, only through the decision of the majority. Here at the very end there crops up again the doubt that Marcuse has sown about the autonomy of the consciousness of the individual.

That Popper's "Open Society" is ultimately devoid of content is a logical consequence of his philosophical and scientific tenets. While for Marcuse science "includes an analysis of tendencies, historical possibilities," and so asserts that social norms and political values are scientifically provable, for Popper there is no certain knowledge, not even in the field of the natural sciences. Our knowledge is critical guesswork. We employ hypotheses to explain problems and the task of the scientist is continually to try to refute them. We tend to trust those hypotheses and theories that withstand such attempts at refutation the longest. They have proved themselves for the time being. Nevertheless, they can be improved on at any time, and we must not rest from attempting this.

In consequence, the conflict between Marcuse and Popper, the neo-Marxist and the social liberal, the "critical rationalist," as Popper would call himself, is rooted above all else in a different theory of science, in a conflicting image of science and its task for man.

### III

As a contemporary whom knowledge of the immorality and inhumanity of the capitalist social order has not converted to Marxism, it seems to me that not only is Marcuse open to criticism from Popper (for example, by the convincing philosophy of science of critical rationalism), but Popper is also open to criticism from Marcuse (for example, from his very much more concrete and subtle diagnosis of our society and the chances in it for self-determination and realization—even if this diagnosis be exaggerated).

I am not sure if there can be a real synthesis be-

tween the contrasting plans of Marcuse and Popper
for the future. But I do believe that the theory that
will form the foundation for a freer and more just
society must borrow elements from the thinking of
*both* philosophers. It is the aim of this confrontation
to set out theoretically their conflicting programs in
order to lay bare points from which an attempt at
synthesis can be made.